Their Paths Are Peace

The Story of Clevelands Cultural Gardens

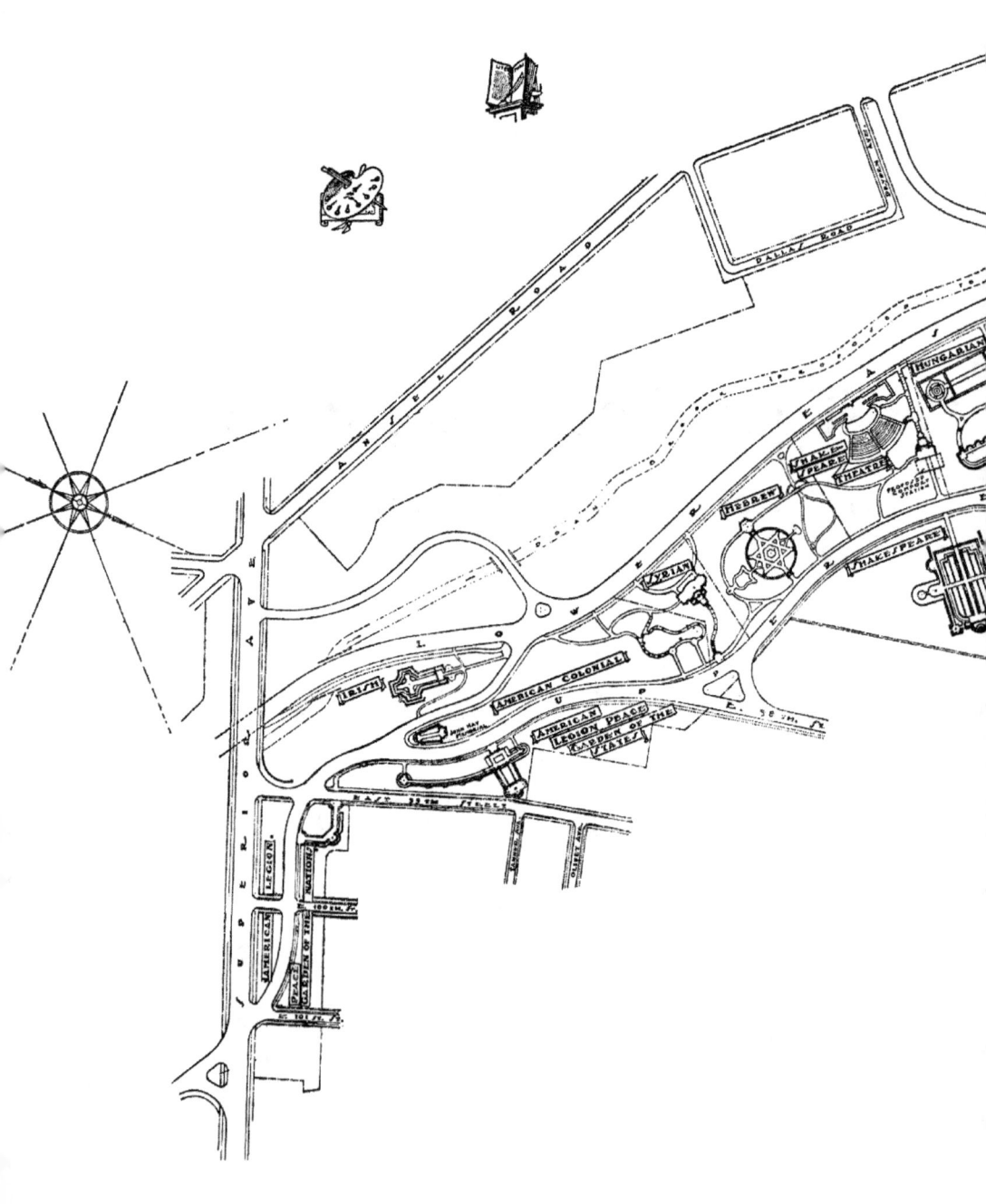

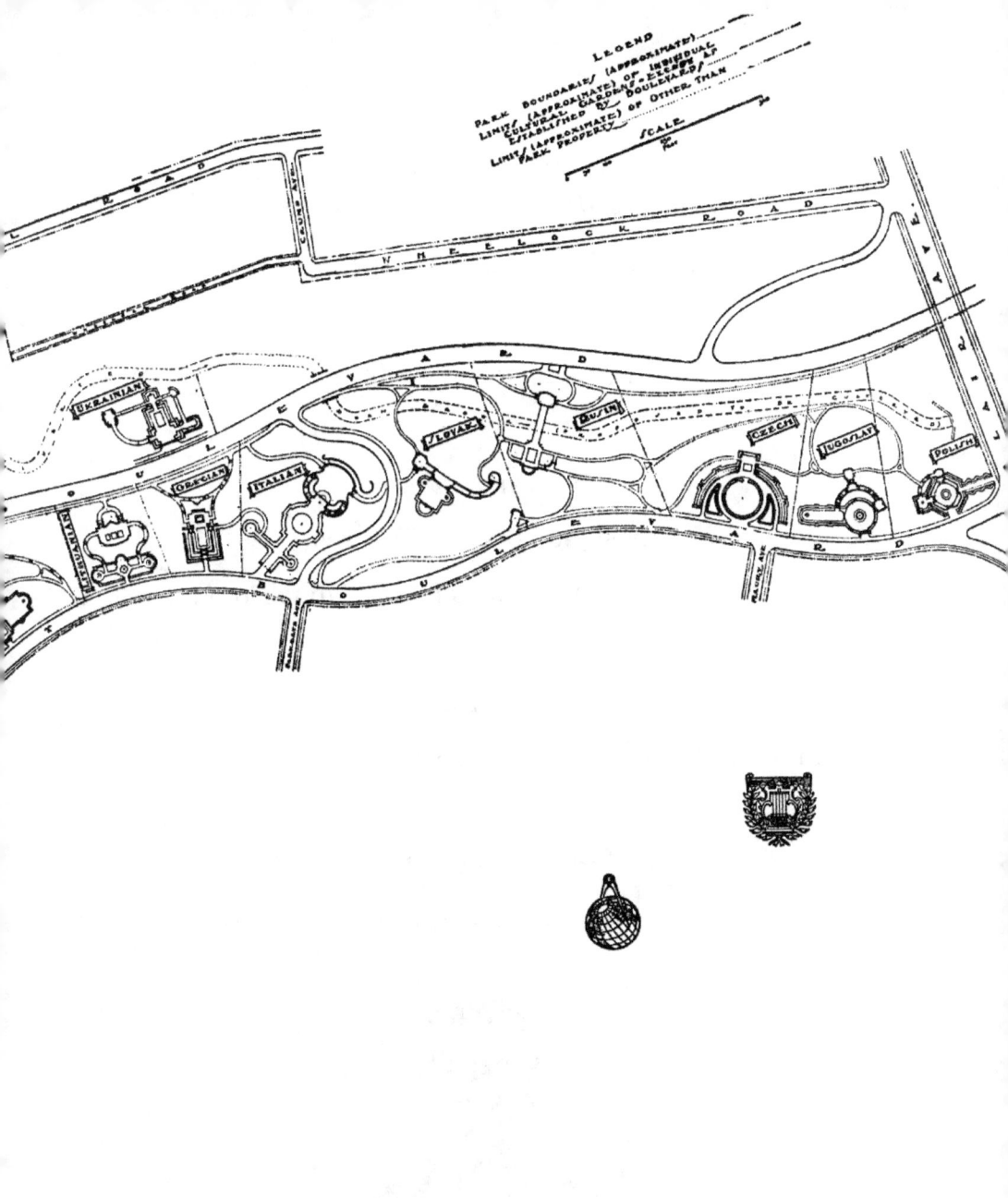

Their Paths Are Peace

The Story of Clevelands Cultural Gardens

65th Anniversary Edition

by Clara Lederer

designed by Jared Bendis

The content of this book is in the Public Doman.

ISBN — 9781626130432

Library of Congress Control Number — 2019954359

Published by ATBOSH Media ltd.

Cleveland, Ohio, USA

http://www.atbosh.com

Their Paths Are Peace

The Story of Clevelands Cultural Gardens

by

Clara Lederer

Originally Published By
The Cleveland Cultural Garden Federation, 1954

Contents

To His Memory (Dedication) 8
As One Out of Many (Foreword) 11
A Refuge of Peace (Introductory Message) 16
Ancestry and Beginnings 19
Through the Years 29
In the True Spirit 35
Leave Hate Behind 39
Their Paths are Peace 45
American Cultural Garden 48
American Legion Peace Gardens 56
Shakespeare Cultural Garden 64
Czech Cultural Garden 72
German Cultural Garden 80
Greek Cultural Garden 88
Hebrew Cultural Garden 96
Hungarian Cultural Garden 108
Irish Cultural Garden 120
Italian Cultural Garden 130
Jugoslav Cultural Garden 138
Lithuanian Cultural. Garden 148
Polish Cultural Garden 158
Rusin Cultural Garden 168
Slovak Cultural Garden 176
Ukrainian Cultural Garden 184
Acknowledgements 191
About the "New" New Edition 193

Airview of Cleveland Cultural Gardens
Photograph by Clyde H. Butler

Charles J. Wolfram

To His Memory

The span of Charles J. Wolframs twenty-five years as president of the Cultural Garden Federation was not merely a period of duties faithfully and loyally performed. It was far more. As president he gave of his strength to the extent of immeasurable sacrifice, for a cause that was near and dear.

Through the early, promotional stage of the Cultural Gardens, he was an inspirational force, participating whole heartedly in the individual gatherings of the constituent organizations of the Federation, not only as officer, but as friend and guide.

The family background of Charles Wolfram is identified with a long line of musicians, teachers and educators. His father and uncle were musicians and stamped upon his lineage as well as upon his own personality there seemed more than a trace of the early Wolfram, the famed poet and Minnesinger of Medieval days, Wolfram von Eschenbach, whose name will be forever linked, because of Wagners opera, with the Tannhauser name and tradition.

Of artistic taste, the Cultural Garden Federation leader, in his early years learned wood engraving. In his youth, the family resided in Akron, later moving to Cleveland where he gained a vast circle of friends, many of whom eagerly joined with him in the establishment and development of the Cultural Gardens.

In Clevelands civic, political and cultural life, he readily gained the confidence of those, who were privileged to be close to him through his active years. He was a charter member of Gilmour Council, Knights of Columbus and his service as president of the American

Equality League, forerunner of the Cultural Garden Federation, as a founder and president, is also noteworthy.

Charles Wolfram was a marl of deep spiritual purpose, devoted to every movement in aid of the cause of human brotherhood. To him, "brotherhood" was not a term for glib usage or phrasing, but an aim that guided his way of life and caused him to be a successful leader in the Cultural Garden enterprise.

In a tribute to Charles Wolfram, delivered at the One World Day gathering, following his death, Judge Louis Petrash said:

"The life of Charles J. Wolfram was one of service—service to others. He has built for himself his own monument—the affection and the respect of all who knew him and his influence on the people who worked with him."

To his memory this book, dealing with the creation and development of a cultural and civic institution which he loved, is dedicated by his friends and co-workers of the Cultural Garden Federation.

May it aid in spreading the doctrine of human understanding and kinship for which his career was an eloquent and moving spokesman.

As One Out of Many

Foreword

Man's earliest memory is not the cave, the dinosaur, the knotted club and the jungle.

Far beyond the dim aeons of savagery, which the delvings of science have reconstructed, is a fair garden eastward in Eden, with tranquil rivers, lofty trees "pleasant to the sight and good for food", and the Voice of the Eternal in the cool of its fading day.

An underlying Love of harmony and peace is ingrained in mans persistent consciousness of that first abode. Before the ages of warfare with nature, before the intertribal and racial feuds is the changeless calm of Paradise.

Try as she may, science cannot obliterate mans recollection of his earliest childhood home. Science spins its tale of ages of tribal fury and rapacity and its summing up is the asseveration of the supremacy of the jungle law of survival of the fittest.

But a higher law graven upon the heart of man is rooted in instincts formed in his earliest placements. Not warfare with nature, nor with fellowman, but an adjustment of the world without, to his own most normal dictates of orderliness and service and harmony, is the eternal and unquenchable will of man. In this direction is the ineffaceable memory of Paradise. Out of these promptings arise mans aspirations to culture, a culture linked forever with the First Garden where nature, not subdued but won in tenderness and sympathy supplied mans every need.

A noted commentator once set forth the belief that men mingle but cultures show no social or gregarious leanings.

Not outwardly perhaps, but there is that within every noble culture that binds it in true understanding to its fellows, indicating a common cultural memory and the common heritage of Eden.

True cultures impose no barriers of race or creed. In fact, their influence is toward mutual understanding and wider sympathy.

Cleveland offers the world a tangible manifestation of this truth. Cosmopolitan to a degree that few cities have been since the far dawn of civilization, Cleveland possesses a cultural institution which exemplifies the oneness of purpose linking great cultures of the world.

In Rockefeller Parkway, along the steep hillsides, between the upper and lower driveways of the East Boulevard, cling the Cleveland Cultural Gardens, with individual units or links, each emblazoning a distinct message of cultural aspiration; each singing a song of the far away homeland of a people that is building anew and in that process of contributing of its own inner cultural and spiritual wealth.

Every gem in this diadem tells not only its own loveliness, but in reflection radiates the color and beauty of its neighbor.

For well over a quarter of a century, pioneers in the Cultural Garden enterprise, and those of later years who have taken up the task, have met monthly in the office of the Mayor, in united consideration of problems, and to work out plans for betterment and future expansion.

Men and women of diversified national and religious backgrounds joined in this communal effort, manifesting true devotion to an effort symbolizing the strength and purpose of American democracy.

As "One out of Many," they, the great city that supported the project from its first inception and the National Government that came forward in an hour when the way seemed darkest and carried the dream to fulfillment, made common cause in this enterprise.

The teachings of Clevelands Cultural. Garden chain are aglow with the spiritual purpose that underlies the way of free and democratic people. For surely, as it was written of true wisdom thousands of years ago;

"Her ways are ways of pleasantness

And all her paths are peace."

—Leo Weidenthal

Their Paths Are Peace

Verdant Symbol

Part One

Mayor Anthony J. Celebrezze

A Refuge of Peace

Introductory Message

Located on a winding trail in a setting, the beauty of which could be created only by the combined efforts of man and nature, the Cultural Gardens of Cleveland symbolize a refuge of peace in a strife-torn world.

The gardens were dedicated in 1939, significantly, the last year of peace since the termination of World War I, The Shakespeare Garden, first of the nineteen presently in the Cultural Garden Plan, was dedicated in 1916 during the midst of this world-wide carnage in which America was engulfed one year later.

Today, the Cultural Gardens of Cleveland demonstrate the unity of the many separate nationality groups who, together, compose the American people. The City of Cleveland can take justifiable pride in the fact that nowhere in the world can a similar testimonial of understanding between peoples be found.

Inscribed on the monument in the American Legion Peace Garden of the Nations are the following words: "In America, peace, understanding, amity, and cooperation among the peoples of all nations," Soil from all parts of the world had been brought to this garden and blended together in a common mixture. The soil coupled with the inscription express the underlying theme or motif of the Cultural Gardens — brotherhood and love of humanity.

The City of Cleveland is a cross section of America. Here we literally have a community of nations. The dream of the American melting pot has never been more clearly demonstrated than in the City of Cleveland where the Cultural Gardens stand as a memorial to the diverse nationalities and cultures of our city.

Mutual understanding, respect and brotherhood are part of the basic tenets of our democratic form of government. From the first day of the founding of the Republic, the inalienable rights of the American people of life, liberty and the pursuit of happiness have been nurtured in the soil of a free land. We have been blessed by Almighty God with a form of government under which we can raise our families in peace and security.

I believe it especially significant that the Gardens are the result of the combined effort of many individuals, groups, and the-City of Cleveland. Each nationality group represented in the series of gardens has raised funds for material and has donated statuary as well as other objects of art of cultural importance. The City of Cleveland has been primarily responsible for the maintenance of the Gardens. This cooperation between the people and government represents the spirit which the Cultural Gardens inculcate in the minds of the people of the world.

I hope and trust that the basic concept behind the Cultural Gardens of Cleveland will provide the necessary impetus in the movement for better understanding among all people, and among all nations throughout the world. When the dream of the Cultural Gardens becomes a reality, we will then be living in a true community of nations under God.

—Anthony J. Celebrezze, Mayor

Ancestry and Beginnings

Witnesses to a great American citys earnest belief in the application of the principles of human brotherhood, Clevelands Cultural Gardens, mirroring the cultural backgrounds of a highly diversified population have steadfastly served as mute, but moving and eloquent spokesmen for the purposes set forth at their dedication more than a quarter of a century ago.

Extending along a mile of wooded hillside, bordering Doan Brook, between Superior and St. Clair Avenues, in Rockefeller Park, the gardens are a product of the united efforts of the Cleveland Cultural Garden Federation, the City of Cleveland and the Federal Government.

World peace, through mutual understanding, is the message they bespeak, and mankinds eternal hope for the dawn of an era of brotherhood in action as well as belief.

Julia Marlowe Reads the Flower Scene at the dedication of the Shakespeare Garden First Event in Cultural Garden Area

Clevelands cosmopolitan citizenry, linked in this effort, has written a message in trees, shrubs, and pathways as a setting to monuments to some sixty world cultural figures, whose inner significance and meaning have not been submerged by the garb of glowing beauty that the years have brought to this unique and notable municipal and civic achievement.

The garden chain now embraces the American Garden, the American Legion Peace Garden of the Nations, the American Legion Peace Garden of the States, the Irish, Hebrew, Shakespeare, Hungarian, German, Ukrainian, Greek, Italian, Slovak, Rusin, Czech, Yugoslav, Lithuanian and Polish Cultural Gardens, each and all, dedicated to the great basic ideas contributed by national cultures upon which our civilization and our American democracy are founded.

> "Gives not the Hawthorn-bush a sweeter shade,
> To shepherds looking on their silly sheep,
> Than doth a rich embroider'd canopy
> To kings that fear their subjects' treachery?"
> Henry VI
>
> **Shakespeare Garden Planting**
> April 14, 1916
>
> Overture - - - Walter's Orchestra
> Introductory - - - -
> Floyd E. Waite, Secretary, Department of Public Service
> Address - Harry L. Davis, Mayor of Cleveland
> Selections - Normal School Glee Club
>   Hark! Hark! the Lark,
>   Who is Sylvia?
>   Director Mrs. Harriet Parsons
> Reading - - - E. H. Sothern
> Selection - Midsummer Night's Dream
>   Orchestra
> Reading - Flower scene from "Winter's Tale"
>   Julia Marlowe
> Planting Excercises - Miss Marlowe and Mr. Sothern
>   Direction John Boddy, City Forester

The First Program

The Cultural Gardens declare today, as they did at their founding, that faith and hope, rooted in past heritages, are the realities of the future.

Cleveland had its Shakespeare Garden ten years before the Cultural Garden development came into being. The establishment of this garden in 1916, the year of the 300th anniversary of the death of Shakespeare, suggested to Leo Weidenthal, Cleveland newspaperman who had been active is the Shakespeare commemorative event, that this cultural project standing alone, failed to present the entire picture of the cultural backgrounds of Clevelands great body of citizens. It was further his belief, that with the completion of the picture, a panorama would he enfolded to stand as a symbol of democracy and brotherhood.

Due to the vision and untiring efforts of the Late Charles J. Wolfram, who was to serve as president of the Cultural Garden Federation for twenty-five years, and, Mrs. Jennie K. Zwick, civic leader and the Federations first executive secretary, the project safely surmounted earliest visionary stages and gradually assumed shape and being. In this transition, the City of Cleveland, then under the guidance of William R. Hopkins as city manager, played an active and far reaching part. City Manager Hopkins became interested in the project in its formative stage and was instrumental in securing aid for its development.

That Cleveland was prepared for such an enterprise and awake to its possibilities and meanings, was due, in a large measure, to two organizations which had been formed for purposes of good-will and civic cooperation among citizens of various national backgrounds. One of these, the Civic Progreso League, destined to become the immediate predecessor of the organization later formed for the direct purpose of promoting the Cultural Gardens, was founded in 1925, with Charles J. Wolfram as president, Leo Weidenthal as honorary president, Mrs. Jennie K. Zwick as executive secretary, Anton Grdina as treasurer and Mrs. Anna

Mokris as recording secretary and historian. It was a federation of nationality groups whose purpose was to foster the spirit of good will and fellowship among men, to weld harmony among Clevelanders of diverse origin, and to promote good citizenship.

Sidney Wilson, Ethel Barrymore, City Manager Hopkins

The other group, with a strikingly similar purpose, was the American Equality League, many of whose organizers were active in the Civic Progress League and later in the establishment of the Cultural Garden League.

The purpose of the American Equality League, as set forth in its Constitution, was "to create and promote a spirit of brotherhood, helpfulness and cooperation among all American people without regard to race, creed or origin, with a profound reverence for the Constitution of the United States of America and its institutions."

Because of this feeling of friendship and goodwill among the various groups of Cleveland, the task of the earliest organizers and promoters of the Cultural Garden enterprise, was lightened in no small degree. When the new development occurred in the life of the Civic Progress League, there was no break.

The Cultural Garden League, succeeding the Civic Progress League, came into being in the year 1926 with Charles J. Wolfram as president, Jennie K. Zwick as executive secretary, Mrs. Anna Mokris as secretary and Leo Weidenthal as honorary president.

As successor to the Civic Progress League, the newly established body thus stated its four-fold aim: "to encourage friendly intercourse, to beautify our city parks, to memorialize our culture heroes and to inculcate appreciation of our cultures."

The Shakespeare Garden had long since become an established city institution when the pioneers began their task of bringing reality to the Cultural Garden idea. Creation of the first garden unit organization was undertaken by Mrs. Zwick and it was an historic moment in the life of the League, when Chaim Nachman Bialik, hailed by Hebraists as the true successor to Judah ha-Levi, visiting Cleveland as guest of honor, on May 5, 1926, planted three Cedars of Lebanon at the future site selected for the Hebrew Cultural Garden.

While this was the earliest formal recognition of the project, under the garden chain plan, in reality, there was an ancestral ceremony at the dedication of the Shakespeare Garden site, April 14, 1916, when the renowned Shakespearean actress, Julia Marlowe and her husband, the famed actor, E. H. Sothern planted American elms, marking the place selected as the entrance to the then yet-to-be Shakespeare Garden.

Miss Marlowe chose as her contribution to the program, a reading of a portion of the flower scene from Shakespeares "Winters Tale". Cleveland, under the spell of her reading, became a spot near the "Seacoast of Bohemia" with Perdita extolling in Shakespeares richest phrases, the glorious beauty of the flowers that fell from the hands of frighted Proserpina in the dim mythland of long, long ago.

Mayor Davis, E. H. Sothern, Julia Marlowe

Chaim Nachman Bialik, Rabbi Solomon Goldman, City Manager Hopkins

Official city recognition of the Cultural Gardens of Cleveland, became a reality on May 9, 1927 with the passage of the following ordinance by the Cleveland City Council:

"An ordinance to set aside a part of Rockefeller Parkway for sculptural tributes to poets and other cultural leaders, and for special landscape and garden development.

"Whereas, the department of parks in the City of Cleveland in the year 1916, for the purpose of commemorating the 300th anniversary of the death of William Shakespeare, did lay out and establish a garden now commonly known as the Shakespeare Garden in Rockefeller Parkway;

"Whereas, at various times since 1916 there have been planted in said Shakespeare Garden, trees and other plantings of great sentimental and historical value, which have materially enhanced the attractiveness and beauty of said garden and made it a feature of the city park development;

"Whereas, upon tracts adjoining said Shakespeare Garden there has been constructed a gateway in memory of the late Marie Bruot and an outdoor theatre, and in addition thereto, a series of plantings have been grouped that will serve as a nucleus of a Hebrew Garden; now, therefore,

"Be it ordained by the Council of the City of Cleveland:

"Section 1. That in view of the improvements heretofore installed and now existing in Rockefeller Parkway, and with a view to perpetuating the sentimental and historical associations thereby established, all that portion of Rockefeller Parkway lying between Superior Avenue on the south and Parkgate Hill east of the lower drive on the north, be and the same is hereby designated The Poets Corner.

"Section 2, That said The Poets Corner be subdivided into units and that the following named units are located and bounded as described in the following sections,

"Section 3. Shakespeare Garden: That portion of Rockefeller Parkway lying east of the upper drive and between North Boulevard and East 98th Street shall be designated The Shakespeare Garden.

"Section 4. Shakespeare Garden Theatre. That portion of Rockefeller Parkway between the upper and lower drives and bounded on the north by a line 25 feet northerly from and parallel with the main axis of the

Shakespeare Garden, extended westerly; and bounded on the south by a line 330 feet southerly from said northerly boundary line and parallel therewith shall be designated the Shakespeare Garden Theatre.

"Section 5. Hebrew Garden. That portion of Rockefeller Parkway between the upper and lower drives bounded on the north by a line 330 feet southerly from and parallel with the main axis of the Shakespeare Garden, extended westerly and bounded on the south by a line 860 feet southerly from and parallel with the northerly boundary line last above described shall be designated the Hebrew Garden.

"Section 6. This ordinance shall be in force and take effect from and after the earliest period allowed by law,"

The ordinance became effective June 19, 1927.

The Poets Corner in later years was to become the Cultural Gardens, and one of the earliest developments, the Shakespeare Garden Theatre, named in the ordinance, though it was the scene of a beautiful presentation of Shakespeares "Mid-Summer Nights Dream" in 1926, the occasion being a feature of the celebration of the one hundredth anniversary of Western Reserve University, came into gradual disuse because of technical presentation difficulties. The Bruot Gate, erected in memory of L. Bruot, for many years, teacher of English speech and director of many school productions of Shakespeare plays at Central High School, still forms the lower Boulevard entrance to the Shakespeare Garden.

With the development of the Hebrew Garden came the other links of the Garden chain in rapid succession. The Italian, German, Slovak, Polish, Hungarian, Czech, Lithuanian, Jugoslav, Rusin, Irish,

American Legion Peace Garden, American, Ukrainian and Greek Gardens came into being in the immediate years following the acceptance of the development plan.

In many cases, their progress was speeded by unlooked for aid from a new source. The explanation of this and the story of developments of the succeeding years are reserved for later chapters.

These, as did the beginnings, reveal the patient effort and the zeal of the devoted band of Cultural Garden pioneers and later workers and the steady backing of city administrations that have stood by the enterprise with true understanding and sympathy.

Through the Years

Succeeding years brought many companions to the little group named in the original Cultural Garden ordinance.

Following the Hebrew Garden came the German Cultural Garden, not far to the north, which, because of the removal of an heroic monument of Goethe and Schiller from Wade Park to the site chosen for the new link in the garden chain, immediately came into possession of an outstanding work of art as an imposing and dominating sculptural feature.

Governor Frank J. Lausche, Addresses Gathering at Dedication of Lincoln Bust

In an ordinance passed by the City Council, Feb. 17, 1930, the German Garden bore the name, German Poets Garden. It is the mightiest poets and dramatists of Germany who occupy the key points in the German Garden today, namely, Goethe, Schiller, Heine and Lessing.

On August 25 of the same year, an ordinance was passed, adding the Slovak, Italian, Lithuanian and Ukrainian Gardens to the list.

A development of the depression era, the extension of Federal aid to public works through WPA, brought realization of a great Cleveland civic project with swiftness that had been undreamed of by the early pioneers and promoters. The labor costs under the Federal aid plan were defrayed by WPA and the various Garden groups were successful in raising funds for the cost of material, working under the general guidance of the city.

In rapid succession, new garden units came into being. On March 30, 1934, an ordinance was passed, establishing the Hungarian, Polish, Czech and Jugoslav Gardens. To these were added the Rusin, Grecian, Syrian, American, Irish and American Legion Peace Gardens on Jan. 31, 1938.

The Federal contribution to the cost of the Cleveland Cultural Gardens, during the period of WPA reached large proportions. This added to the citys contributions and to the large amounts expended by the individual Cultural Garden groups as sponsors in WPA projects and in the erection of statuary and plaques, has resulted in a total estimated valuation well in excess of $1,250,000.

The art and skill of T. Ashburton Tripp, as landscape architect, and of Frank L. Jirouch as sculptor, served the Cultural Gardens in their earlier stages and later development as well.

At the time of the 25th anniversary celebration of the Cultural Garden Federation, which occurred in 1950, in connection with the Federations One World Day, there were more than fifty monuments and plaques in the various gardens. Those done by Frank L. Jirouch, include busts of Lincoln, Mark Twain, Artemus Ward, John Hay, Alexander Duchnovich; all the busts as well in the Czech Garden the bust of Madame Curie in the

Polish Garden; the bronze plaques and portrait reliefs on the entrance gate to the Ukrainian Garden and the Brotherhood Shrine erected by the Bnai Brith, on the upper boulevard, between the hillside entrance to the Shakespeare Garden and the Hebrew Garden.

Mantell Sun Dial—Shakespeare Garden

In 1936, additional aid was given the project with the creation of a City Division of Landscape Architecture. Under the general supervision of Hugo E. Varga, then director of Parks and Public Properties, a study was made of proposed as well as existing gardens and a unification plan adopted, to bind the units into one general scheme by a series of bordered paths.

This scheme was carried out, thereby enabling the gardens to tell their story with even greater clarity and effectiveness. In fact, so successful was this landscape undertaking, that many visitors including Viscount Halifax, British Ambassador to the United States noted that the Cultural Gardens appeared amid their setting of trees and shrubs, as a single garden, whose elements were mingled in a pattern of harmony and beauty.

Keenly alive to the unity motive of the Cultural Gardens, Guillaume Fatio, Swiss historian and representative of the League of Nations, visited the gardens in 1935 and planted a tree near the Superior Avenue entrance.

"Clevelands Cultural Gardens are accomplishing in their community the same thing that the League of Nations is trying to do for the world," he said in his address.

The League representative who was in Cleveland under the auspices of the Carnegie Endowment for International Peace, to speak for the cause of the League of Nations, stated that the Cleveland Cultural Gardens would serve as a model in miniature for the landscaping of the grounds around the Leagues palace at Geneva, which were to be opened in the summer of that year.

Dedication of Jahn Memorial
German Cultural Garden

Eighteen years after the visit of the Swiss historian, another visitor to the gardens, standing on the spot where the Leagues spokesman had delivered his message of world peace, said: "I will return to Switzerland in the summer for a visit and then I will tell my grandfather that his tree is growing well."

The speaker, Pierre C. Zoelly of Columbus, grandson of the Swiss historian, had come to Cleveland to attend a meeting of the Society of Architectural Historians, and had arranged to visit the Cultural Gardens at the request of his grandfather, then eighty-eight years of age.

Through the years that had elapsed since Guillaume Fatio planted his tree, the Cultural Gardens had continued to tell their story of brotherhood and peace, loyal to the purpose of their founders and to the doctrines of the Nation and the City that had supported their creation and development.

In the True Spirit

Many colorful chapters in the story of Clevelands Cultural Gardens have been of special significance because of mass participation by the groups and because of their close association with the underlying purpose of the gardens.

In this connection, the Cultural Gardens dedication should be stressed. This occasion, embraced the turning over of all of the gardens to the City of Cleveland, with a colorful program including a parade of large representations of the various garden groups, men, women and children in the beautiful garb of their native lands across the sea. This program was given, July 30, 1939.

Of general importance in the story of the gardens is the 25th anniversary celebration which took place, July 19-23, 1950 and included the dedication of the Lincoln Shrine in the American Garden at the Superior Avenue entrance to the gardens. This was held jointly with the celebration of One World Day, an annual event described in a later chapter and was conducted jointly by the Cultural Garden Federation and the Cleveland City Division of Recreation, headed by John S. Nagy as commissioner of recreation. Features of this celebration are noted in a chapter devoted to the American Garden.

A stirring Cultural Garden occasion was the later dedication of the Brotherhood Shrine, with its memorial to the Four American Chaplains who gave their lives that the lives of soldiers on the sinking ship, Dorchester might be saved.

The crowning feature of the dedication of the Cleveland Cultural Gardens which was held on the occasion of the Seventh Worlds Poultry Congress and Exposition was the World Peace Rally which took place at the Music Hall, on the evening of July 30, 1939, with Archbishop Joseph J. Schrembs, Rabbi Rudolph M. Rosenthal of the Temple on the Heights and Dr. Edwin McNeill Poteat of the Euclid Avenue Baptist Church among the speakers. Charles J. Wolfram, president of the Cultural Garden League was chairman.

Brotherhood Shrine—Memorial to the Four Heroic Chaplains

The dedication ceremonies were confined to the program of the afternoon of that day, opening with an early program in the Garden of the Nations of the American Legion Peace Garden. On this occasion occurred the unveiling of the Peace Monument. The address was given by Paul V. McNutt, Federal Security Administrator, Past National Commander of the American Legion and former United States High Commissioner to the Philippine Islands. Then followed an impressive ceremony, the intermingling and depositing of soil from historic shrines of nations of the world in a metal box in the base of the Peace Monument Shrine.

The parade of the various nationality groups and the American Legion to the site of the general dedication ceremony followed. Among the opening features were a roll call of presidents of the Cultural Gardens by Jennie K. Zwick, executive secretary of the League and presentation of the Cultural Gardens to the City of Cleveland by Leo Weidenthal, honorary president. The gardens were accepted in the name of the City by Mayor Harold H. Burton. Karl K. Kitchen, president of the American Legion Peace Garden presented the guest speaker, Paul V. McNutt. His theme was "To the Cause of Brotherhood and Peace."

On October 25, 1953, the Brotherhood Shrine was dedicated in the section adjacent to the Hebrew Garden between the upper and lower level entrances to the Shakespeare Garden, by the Bnai Brith Lodges and chapters of Cleveland as part of their centennial celebration. The shrine is a memorial to the Four Army Chaplains, Reverend George L. Fox, Reverend Clark V. Poling, Father John P. Washington, and Rabbi Alexander D. Goode, whose heroic choice of voluntary death to save their fellow-soldiers during the torpedoing of the U. S. Troopship Dorchester on February 3, 1943, during World War II, endures as one of the most noble deeds in the annals of our country.

The bronze plaque affixed to the granite rostrum depicts the figures of the four chaplains kneeling in prayer before a female figure representing a mother gathering her sons to her. Sculptor Frank pouch was the designer.

Mrs. Lewis W. Phillips, executive secretary of the Cultural Garden Federation, made introductory remarks and presented guests. After the presentation of the Colors by the Catholic War Veterans and the singing of the National Anthem by Samuel C. Levine, cantorial soloist of the Euclid Avenue Temple, the invocation was delivered by Rabbi Earl S. Stone of the Temple, a chaplain in World War H. Judge Albert A. Woldman was master of ceremonies, and Robert Silverman, president of Bnai Brith Inter-Lodge Council, and Mrs. Reuben Glazer, president of the Bnai Br ith Womens Council, made the presentation of the shrine, which was accepted on behalf of the city by John J. Locuoco director of parks and public property.

The Bnai Brith Sol Fetterman Award for accomplishment in the realm of community relations was then made to Leo Weidenthal, president of the Cultural Garden Federation, by Alfred A. Benesch.

Dr. Daniel Poling of Philadelphia, editor of the Christian Herald and father of Chaplain Clark V. Poling, one of the hero chaplains, was principal speaker. "We must live together in the spirit of our soldiers dying," he said. "The uniqueness of our freedom is our unity, which strengthens loyalty."

Greetings were extended by Father Lawrence Wolfe of the Holy Family Church, a colonel in the U. S. Army Chaplain Corps.

This monument to two Protestant ministers, a priest, and a rabbi, honors all faiths, and is a perpetual demonstration of interfaith brotherhood in the true spirit of the Cultural Gardens.

Leave Hate Behind

Every year on the Sunday nearest July 22nd, Cleveland Founders Day, One World Day is celebrated.

Dedicated to the idea of the Cultural Gardens — that all nationalities can work together in harmony— One World Day is a demonstration in colorful pageantry enriched by the unique folk art contribution of each national culture.

One World Day has been celebrated since 1946. In 1947, a resolution was offered, stating that, acting in accordance with the ideals which had inspired the United Nations, the Cultural Garden League undertook the observance of an annual One World Day in Cleveland. It was further resolved that a copy be sent to the United Nations with the hope that they establish an annual international One World Day to be observed by all peoples in furtherance of a spirit of world-wide amity and peace. The resolution was adopted by unanimous vote on the occasion of the second observance of One World Day, July 20, 1947.

These celebrations which have been conducted annually under the direction of a committee headed by

Mrs. Lewis W. Phillips, are characterized by the participation of groups resplendent in their beautiful costumes of the Old World in the natural amphitheatre in the Jugoslav Garden. The programs open with the advancing of the Colors by the American Legion Guard. The singing of the National Anthem and other patriotic songs is led by some outstanding choral group of the city, and music of the nationality units fills gardens with old world melodies. In the amphitheatre, addresses are delivered by nationally known cultural and political figures, and folk songs and dances are offered by gifted exponents of various national cultures. Thus, one span of a radiant Sunday afternoon may comprise a Hungarian Czardas, an Irish jig and ballad, chants by a Greek Orthodox choir, a Polish mazurka, Slovenian hymns, a Ukrainian harvest dance, an Italian tarantella, a German polka, Palestinian folk dances from the Holy Land, and will terminate with a grand finale of the singing of "God Bless America" by all the groups present. These programs are followed by conducted tours of the garden chain, and by exhibits of folk art, in the various individual gardens.

In 1950, the One World Day observance marked the 25th anniversary of the founding of the Cultural Gardens. The parade on this occasion was led by drummers and fifer representing the famous figures in the "Spirit of 76." Clevelanders wearing traditional costumes marched in the Old American, Czech, German, Dutch, Greek, French, Chinese, Japanese, Hungarian, Hebrew, Irish, Lithuanian, Polish, Roumanian, Rusin, Russian, Norwegian, Danish, Finnish, Swedish, Scotch, Slovak, English, Welsh, Ukrainian, and Lebanese groups. Lieutenant Colonel Jack Persky was marshal of the parade, the units of which were welcomed at the Jugoslav Garden by a Slovene group in native costume. Charles J. Wolfram, then president of the Cultural

Garden League, traced the history of the gardens development. Mayor Thomas A. Burke hailed the garden movement as proof that people of differing national backgrounds can live together in unity. Historical characters from the pageant, including Joshua and Isaiah, were introduced. The program concluded in the Hungarian Garden with the unveiling of a bust of the Hungarian tragic poet, Imre Madach

Dr. Joseph Remenyi and the Reverend Andor Leffler were principal speakers, and prayers were offered by Dr. Stephen Szabo and the Reverend Eugene Tabakovich, the three divines representing respectively the Evangelical Lutheran, Hungarian Reformed, and Catholic faiths. Congressman Frances P. Bolton came from Washington expressly to participate in this affair.

In 1952, the Cleveland Chamber of Commerce became joint sponsor of One World Day, together with the Cultural Garden Federation and the city recreation department. Dr. John S. Millis, president of Western Reserve University, in the principal address called Cleveland a melting pot of nationalities and a living demonstration of the American dream of human brotherhood. "We are all heirs to a common culture," he said further. "We are all the beneficiaries of the literature of science, music, art, and the law of all nations. The university is the trustee of this common knowledge. Western Reserve University is a testament of the belief in One World and of the opportunity to preserve the culture of all races and all nationalities." The program, which began with a flag-raising ceremony, and included national songs and dances, ended with a tour of the gardens conducted by George N. Kalkas, vice-president of the Cultural Garden Federation.

Dedication of Jugoslav Cultural Garden

The 1953 One World Day observance was a gala civic event dedicated to the Ohio Sesquicentennial. Curtis Lee Smith, president of the Cleveland Chamber of Commerce, said that Clevelands creation of its own "One World" of nationality groups should serve as an example to men and women in other parts of the country and of the world. The pageant symbolized the contributions of the various nationality groups to the development of Cleveland and of Ohio. Indians, Moravian missionaries, and Moses Cleaveland and his band of settlers from New England, figured in the procession. An Indian dance and an Hungarian folk dance especially delighted the crowd. The arrival of Irish. German, Hebrew, Czech, Hungarian, Polish, Slovak, Italian, Slovene, Lithuanian, Russian, Ukrainian, Greek, and Finnish settlers was dramatized. The pageant closed with a representation of the Statue of Liberty by Miss Lily P. Volosin, a member of the board of directors of the Cultural Garden Federation. Spirited music was furnished by the Cleveland Municipal Band, directed by Milton W. Foy.

In the direction of this program, as in past previous events, Mrs. Winifred M. Hodges, superintendent of the Bureau of Music, City Division of

Recreation, cooperated actively with the Garden Federation.

Earliest observances of One World Day were held on the grounds at the foot of the hill west of the lower East Boulevard, used for baseball games. Later, the event was transferred to the Slovak Garden, and still later, the lower portion of the Jugoslav Garden, which forms a perfect amphitheatre, was chosen as the site for the annual observance.

During the year of the celebration of Clevelands sesquicentennial, a featured event was a parade of floats, in which the Cultural Garden units were participants, depicting in beautiful floral designs the cultural backgrounds of the various elements of Clevelands population.

A novel feature of the 1954 observance was an array of booths on the slopes leading to the lowest portion of the amphitheatre. Objects characteristic of Old World folk art were displayed.

Suggested as a suitable inscription for the entrance to the Cultural Gardens has been a paraphrase from Dante: "Leave hate behind, all ye who enter here." In keeping with this sentiment, One World Day accentuates the purpose for which the Cultural Gardens were created, and sets forth the meaning of their existence.

Their Paths are Peace

The Cultural Gardens constitute a verdant symbol of the perpetual renewal of the human spirit through past cultures and future aspirations.

As divergent elements of an harmonious whole, they represent democracy and brotherhood as set forth in the American ideal.

They are testimony to the faith of their founders that in the visions of poet and prophet, of artist and musician, are after all to be found the supreme realities of history, and that it is the dreams of men which forge the destinies of nations.

If, as has been said, imagination rules the world, clear recognition of the place of those who have consistently envisioned the upbuilding of human civilization, will bring speedier realization of their dream and ultimate fulfillment.

The "Choir Invisible, whose music is the gladness of the world," may be heard without jarring, discordant influences in the Cleveland Cultural Gardens.

Like a green diadem crowning the trail of hope to world peace, these gardens recall Emersons lines on the Parthenon and other man-made masterpieces of the earth:

"For out of Thoughts interior sphere
These wonders rose to upper air;
And Nature gladly gave them place,
Adopted them into her race;
And granted them an equal date
With Andes and with Ararat."

The ways of Clevelands Cultural Gardens are ways of pleasantness. All their paths bespeak the peace of a world without hate, without fear, without mistrust, without greed, seeking only the com-mon good in the light of an eternal day.

Cleveland—proud to possess this true garden spot of the nation where ideas and foliage flourish in unison—possesses it, however, only in the geographical sense. For in the more profound sense of dedication to cosmopolitan friendship and universal culture, the Cultural Gardens of Cleveland belong to America and to the world.

Links In The Chain

History of the Cultural Gardens

Part Two

Lincoln Memorial
City of Cleveland Photograph

American Cultural Garden

The American Cultural Garden is located west of the upper Boulevard just north of the Superior Avenue intersection. It is planted informally with native varieties of trees, shrubs, and vines.

In 1933 the administration of the Cleveland Council Parent Teachers Association, by unanimous resolution voted to support the American Garden project. Mrs. Norma Wulff, then president of the P.T.A. Council, appointed Mrs. Anna Ochs as chairman of the American Garden project. Mrs. Jennie K. Zwick was invited to speak before the P.T.A. and described in detail the plan for the American Garden.

The future site of the American Garden was dedicated by the Parent Teachers Association Council on May 24, 1935. Mrs. Norma Wulff presided and introduced Mrs. Anna Ochs. Cleveland school children participated in the program with American folk dancing, and the P.T.A. Mothersingers sang American folk songs, including those of Stephen Foster. Charles L. Lake, then superintendent of schools, extended greetings. School bands played the National Anthem and "America the Beautiful."

Here on December 6, 1935, a bronze bust of Mark Twain, the work of Frank L. Jirouch, and bought with pennies given by the Cuyahoga County public school children, was unveiled upon the 100th anniversary of the authors birth. Mark Twain, pseudonym of Samuel Langhorn Clemens (1835-1910), most famous for his works, Tom Sawyer and Huckleberry Finn, was the first American to be commemorated in the Cultural Gardens. The bust was accepted by the late Hugo E. Varga, parks director. A program followed at the Cleveland Museum of Art. Speakers included Mr. E. J. Bryan, superintendent of Cuyahoga County Schools; Charles Wolfram, at that time president of the Cultural Gardens League; Mayor Harold H. Burton; Dr. A. Caswell Ellis, director of Cleveland College; Mr. Ted Robinson, the Cleveland Plain Dealers "Philosopher of Folly"; and Mr. Robert K. Beck, president of the County Board of Education. The program also included songs by Public School pupils, under the direction of Zoe Long Fouts, and a skit based on the works of Mark Twain.

On October 27, 1938, Mark Twains daughter, Clara, at that time Madame Ossip Gabrilowitsch, placed a wreath at the Twain bust.

On July 23, 1939, a bust of John Hay (1838-1905), American statesman and author, secretary to

Abraham Lincoln, and Secretary of State from 1898 to 1905, was dedicated. The bust was presented to the American Garden by the Bnai Brith organization, in recognition of John Hays great service in defense of European Jewry against the Russian and Roumanian persecutions of the 19th century, which he regarded as a major matter of international concern. As a young attorney, he married Clara Stone, daughter of Amasa Stone, of Cleveland, and was a resident of Cleveland for about ten years. He is buried in Lake View Cemetery, near the tomb of President Garfield. The inscription on the John Hay monument in the American Garden reads as follows:

"Companion and biographer of Lincoln, ambassador to Great Britain; Secretary of State under McKinley and Roosevelt, author, journalist. Presented by Bnai Brith on the 100th anniversary of the birth of John Hay, in recognition of his championship of the cause of the persecuted, and his merited distinction as a statesman of good will."

Daughter of Mark Twain (the former Clara Clemens) at the Twain Memorial

Speakers at the John Hay dedication ceremony were Mayor Harold H. Burton, Rabbi Armond E. Cohen, Philmore J. Haber, Charles J. Wolfram, and Harold T. Clark. The Hay bust is the work of Frank L. Jirouch.

On August 2, 1948, a bust of Artemus Ward (183 44 867) , pen name of Charles Farrar Browne, noted lecturer and humorist, and in 1859 a member of the Cleveland Plain Dealer staff, was given to the city by the Plain Dealer. The work of Sculptor Frank Jirouch, the bust was presented to the City of Cleveland by William G. Vorpe, Sunday editor of the Cleveland Plain Dealer on behalf of Paul Bellamy, editor-in-chief. Mayor Thomas A. Burke accepted the bust for the city, Charles J, Wolfram gratefully acknowledged it as a notable addition to the other Cultural Garden memorials, and Donald Lybarger, president of the Early Settlers Association, was the principal speaker in a talk paying tribute to Wards career. At the conclusion of the dedication, the bust was unveiled by Miss Patricia Gray, assistant society editor of the Cleveland Plain Dealer and great-granddaughter of A. N. Gray, co-founder of the Plain Dealer. William Ganson Rose was master of ceremonies.

Children of Cuyahoga County Schools Gather at Dedication of Mark Twain Memorial

At the apex of the hillside triangle which forms the entrance to the American Garden stands a bronze bust of Abraham Lincoln (1809-1865), sixteenth

President of the United States known as the "Great Emancipator." Also the work of Sculptor Frank L. Jirouch, the bust was dedicated on July 22, 1950, on the occasion of the celebration of the 25th anniversary of the founding of the Cultural Gardens. The bust was made possible by the Peter -Witt memorial fund." Principal speakers at the dedication were Governor Frank J. Lausche, Nathaniel R. Howard, editor of the Cleveland News, and Albert A. Waldman, vice-president of the Abraham Lincoln Association of Ohio.

Artemus Ward

"Like Lincoln, we must face unflinchingly the task Fate set before us," said Governor Lausche, in his address. Mr. Howard, in a tribute to Peter Witt, former councilman and civic leader, said that the late Clevelander admired Lincoln for his qualities of courage and patience, for his simple faith in the American people, and for his strength as a constitutional revolutionist. "Now is a time when we can all stand a little honest hero worship,- Mr. Howard added.

Mr. Waldman described Lincolns visit to Cleveland on his way to Washington for his 1861 inauguration. The Lincoln bust was unveiled by Peter Witts granddaughter, Miss Sally Cummins.

On June 11, 1951, the dedication of the completed Lincoln shrine took place. Historian William Ganson Rose spoke, paying tribute to Lincoln, John .1-lay, George Washington, Artermus Ward, and other famous Americans. Mayor Thomas A. Burke also spoke, paying tribute to the generous efforts and activities of Charles Wolfram and Leo Weidenthal, and other Federation leaders. George Kalkas was program chairman. The pedestal upon which rests the sculptured head was donated by the city. The inscription upon it reads:

"Erected in memory of Peter Witt

Devoted public servant who sought light and guidance from the ideals of the Great Emancipator. 1869-1948"

Set in the Lincoln shrine to the right of the bust is an ornamental bronze tablet inscribed with the complete Gettysburg Address, and signed with a reproduction of the authors autograph—A. Lincoln. The plaque, with stone mounting, was a joint gift of A. L. Maresh, noted Lincoln collector, and General Julius Klein, who presented the mounting through the Jewish War Veterans.

Active chairmanship has been shared by Mrs. Anna M. Ochs and Mrs. Norma Wulff, under whose presidency in later years the work of the reorganization of the American Garden on a broad scale has been in progress. Mrs. Ochs is vice-president.

Typical of our national culture which it represents, in the Cultural Gardens chain, the American Garden, in its picturesque and flourishing forest setting, confidently awaits additions of other leaders in the nations life.

John Hay

American Legion Peace Garden
City of Cleveland Photograph

American Legion Peace Garden

The American Legion Peace Gardens are located at the southern entrance to the Garden chain, east of upper East Boulevard, where Rockefeller Park joins Superior Avenue. They are divided into two sections, one being devoted to the nations and the other to the United States.

The chief feature of the Garden of the Nations is a semi-circular, high-backed seat of classical design, surmounted by the head of a beautiful woman, symbolizing peace, and done in Tennessee marble by Henry Herring. A bronze tablet affixed to the monument bears the inscription, "Dedicated to the Cause of Brotherhood and Peace on the occasion of International

Peace Day of the 7th Worlds Poultry Congress and Exposition, July 30, 1939," in honor of the official dedication of this garden. Also upon that occasion, the soil from twenty-eight nations was deposited by ambassadors and consular representatives of those nations in a marble crypt at the base of the monument, and the bronze tablet now covering it is inscribed,

> "September 20, 1936.
>
> The American Legion Peace Gardens The Nations
>
> Here in soil from historic shrines of the Nations of the World, are planted trees to create the American Legion Peace Gardens. May the intermingled soil of the nations symbolize the united effort of their peoples as they advance to a better understanding. These gardens planned by men who know the horrors of war, are dedicated to the brotherhood of man and peace throughout the world.
>
> Established by The American Legion 1936 Convention Corporation of Cleveland and dedicated by Ray Murphy, National Commander, The American Legion."

The author of the tablet was Legionnaire Glen Campbell and the sculptor was Frank L. Jirouch.

The section devoted to the United States and known as The American Legion Peace Garden of the States lies north of the Garden of Nations on the east side of the upper drive. It is marked by a stone pedestal upon which is affixed a bronze tablet similar in design and inscription to the one dedicated to the nations. It bears the following inscription:

> "September 20, 1936.
>
> The American Legion Peace Gardens
>
> The United States

Here in soil from historic shrines of the States of the Union, are planted trees to create The American Legion Peace Gardens. May the intermingled soil of the States symbolize the national unity which constitutes the strength of our great Republic. These gardens, planned by men who know the horrors of war, are dedicated to the brotherhood of man and peace throughout the world.

Established by The American Legion 1936 Convention Corporation of Cleveland and dedicated by Ray Murphy, National Commander, The American Legion."

In this section there is also a bust of George Washington, presented by the American Legion and unveiled on July 4, 1943. Brigadier General Robert L. Denig, U. S. M.C., delivered the principal address.

Participation of the American Legion in Cultural Gardens activity began in 1935, when the late Karl K. Kitchen, executive vice-president of the American Legion Convention Corporation, conferred with Mrs. Jennie K. Zwick, at that time secretary of the Cultural Garden League.

The American Legion and its Auxiliaries were at that time and from the end of World War I members in an international society organized to promote world peace and known under the coined French name of "Fidac" otherwise known as the Federation Interalliee des Anciens Combattants. Fidac had the following nations as members: United States, Great Britain, France, Belgium, Portugal, Italy, Roumania, Poland, Czechoslovakia, Jugoslavia and Greece. Fidac was then represented by Dorothy B. Persky of the American Legion Auxiliaries of Cuyahoga County and was arranging a meeting of all the delegates from our European Allies at the National Convention of the

American Legion in September 1936, and Fidac was to take part in the dedication ceremonies of the American Legion Peace Gardens during the Convention.

Peace

Ordinances were passed by the City Council on November 18, 1935, and August 31, 1936, respectively, designating specific areas along Rockefeller Parkway just north of Superior Avenue, for the future American Legion Peace Gardens.

The dedication of these gardens took place on September 20, 1936, during the American Legion Convention in Cleveland. Participating in ceremonies were the following members of the Legion: Mayor Harold H. Burton, who accepted the new addition to the Cultural Garden chain on behalf of the city Ray Murphy, national commander, who delivered the dedicatory address Karl K. Kitchen, executive vice-president of the Convention Corporation Father Kennedy, national chaplain Glen Campbell, chairman of the entertainment committee Ralph Ammerman, master of ceremonies and Jack A. Persky of the Convention Corporation. The bronze tablet to the nations was unveiled, and delegates from allied nations during the late wars placed soil from their native shrines at the foot of the monument to the nations, symbolizing the united efforts of the nations for peace.

Many of the members of the American Legion who had taken part in the founding and dedication of the Peace Gardens in 1936, took an active part in planning and conduction the 7th World Poultry Congress which took place in Cleveland in July of 1939. At this time occurred the mass dedication of the entire Cultural Gardens chain, when Paul V. McNutt, past national commander of the American Legion gave the principal address.

Dedication of John Hay Memorial at Exercises on the Mall. Mayor Burton, Mrs. Robert H. Bishop, Clarence Hay, W.G. Mather, P.J. Haber, Harold T. Clark, Frank L. Jirouch

After the establishment of the new nation of Israel in 1948, the late Municipal Court Judge Lewis Drucker, visited Israel for the purpose of obtaining sacred soil to be added to that of other nations in the Peace Gardens crypt. This was accomplished on October 23, 1949, when, in an impressive ceremony, the crypt was opened to accept the soil of Israel. -

Karl K. Kitchen was a member of the board of trustees of the Cultural Garden League from the inception of the American Legion Peace Gardens in 1936 until the time of his death in 1949. He was assisted by Jack A. Persky, a former county commander of the American Legion, and by Dorothy B. Persky of the American Legion Auxiliary. Jack A. Persky succeeded Mr. Kitchen as the American Legion representative in the Cultural Gardens Federation.

The American Legion which is composed of men and woman of every national origin, every religion, and every degree of culture found in the United States was founded in 1919 and by its preamble the members are associated together for God and Country and to carry out its many objectives they are pledged to combat the autocracy of both the classes and the masses, to promote peace and good will on earth and to safeguard and transmit to posterity the principles of justice, freedom and democracy. These concepts are the embodiment of the spirit and purpose of the Nationality Gardens in the Cleveland Cultural Garden Federation.

At the present writing, plans are being developed for the future embellishment of the American Legion Peace Gardens with tablets and monuments consecrated to harmony among nations and to the advancement of the American way of life.

Thus, the story of the Peace Gardens is the story of the American Legions prominent role in Cultural Gardens history, a role in keeping with the Legions fighting spirit in the cause of brotherhood and peace.

Shakespeare Garden
City of Cleveland Photograph

Shakespeare Garden

The Shakespeare Garden, ancestor of the Cultural Gardens, is Elizabethan in mood and pattern.

At the entrance are gateposts of English design and the garden boundaries are defined with hedges. The central flagstone walk is lined with multi-hued border plantings, and, together with other her-bordered paths, converging on a bust of Shakespeare flanked by trees. A mulberry tree grows here from cutting sent by the late Sir Sidney Lee, famed Shakespearean critic, from the mulberry, Shakespeare himself planted at New Place, in Stratford. In addition to elms planted by E. H. Sothen and Julia Marlowe, the garden is adorned with oaks planted by the Irish poet, William Butler Yeats, and by

Phyllis Neilson Terry, niece of Ellen Terry a circular bed of roses (Shakespeares favorite flower) sent by the Mayor of Verona, from the traditional tomb of Juliet Birnam Wood sycamore maples transplanted from Scotland, and several other representative English forest trees. The Byzantine sundial was presented by the distinguished actor, Robert Mantell. Also formerly included were jars planted with ivy and flowers by Sir Herbert Beerbohm Tree, Rabindranath Tagore—the "Shakespeare of India"—and Sarah Bernhardt.

The garden plot was laid out under the direction of City Forester John Boddy, and was copiously planted with hawthorn, daffodils, violets, fleurs-de-lis, daisies, pansies, and columbine—the flowers given immortality in the poetry of Shakespeare.

The Shakespeare Garden inaugural exercises took place on April 14th, 1916, the tercentenary year, on the upper boulevard near the garden entrance. E. H. Sothen and Julia Marlowe were guests of honor. After speeches of welcome by city officials and Mayor Harry L. Davis, the orchestra played selections from Mendelssohns "Midsummer Nights Dream," and the Normal School Glee Club sang choral setting of "Hark, Hark, the Lark" and "Who Is Sylvia?" A group of high school pupils in Elizabethan costume escorted the guests to the garden entrance and stood guard during the planting of the dedicatory elms. In his formal talk, Mr. Sothen urged storytelling days for children in the public parks. Miss Marlowe climaxed the proceedings by her readings of Perditas flower scene from "Winters Tale," the 54th Sonnet of Shakespeare, and verses from the Star Spangled Banner. Her leading of all present in the singing of the National Anthem brought the impressive event to a close.

Shakespeare

A limestone bust of the poet, the work of Joseph Motto and Stephen Rebeck, preceded a bronze bust, recently placed in the garden. Speakers at the formal dedication of the bust on October 21, 1916, were Alex Bernstein, director of public service, William Raddatz, organizer of the Shakespeare Memorial Committee and president of the Cleveland Advertising Club, and Judge Willis Vickery, Shakespeare student and collector.

Willows flanking the fountain dais were planted by William Faversham and Daniel Frohman. Vachel Lindsay, planted a poplar and recited his own Shakespeare tribute. Novelist Hugh Walpole also planted a tree here. Notable joint visits to the garden were those of Edwin Markham, author of "The Man With the Hoe," and Aline Kilmer, widow of the soldier poet, Joyce Kilmer, in 1919 and of the actor, Otis Skinner and the humorist, Stephen Leacock. David Belasco came to plant two junipers, and Effie Ellsler, whose early triumphs occurred on the stage of Clevelands Academy of Music, planted a maple near the Mantell sundial. Jane Cowl, during her Cleveland "Juliet" engagement, planted an elm near Juliets rose-bed. Two eminent Cleveland writers, Edmund Vance Cooke, poet, and Carl Robertson, nature writer, also planted trees.

The entrance gate, giving access to the upper hillside garden from the lower boulevard, was erected in 1925 as a memorial to Marie Leah Bruot, a teacher at Clevelands Central High School. It symbolizes her long service as a gateway to Shakespeare appreciation for many Clevelanders. The stone and iron gate was designed by City Architect Herman Kregelius. George Barber headed the memorial committee.

In 1926 the renowned Shakespeare mulberry was enclosed by a circular bench donated by the Shakespeare Society, and dedicated on the poets birthday by the Federation of Womens Clubs.

The Shakespeare Mulberry

On June 15th and 16th, 1926, "A Midsummer Nights Dream" was presented by members of the drama clubs of Western Reserve University, in a natural amphitheatre formed by the slopes between the upper and lower boulevards. Ethel Barrymore planted the key hawthorn of the bushes set out as a stage background.

On June 13th and 14th of 1936, "The Tempest" was given by the Baldwin Wallace College Players of Berea, under the auspices of the Daughters of the British Empire, and jointly sponsored by the Cultural Garden League and the Parks Department of Cleveland.

Since 1931 the Daughters of the British Empire have been the active Shakespeare Garden group, with Mrs. G. W. Mercer as leader. Notable tree-plantings under their sponsorship included a tribute to the Bicentennial of George Washington on May 24, 1932 a planting in honor of Alfred, Lord Tennyson, on the 125th anniversary of his birth, August 6, 1934 a seedling from the Royal Forest, England, received May 12, 1937, commemorating the coronation of the late King George the Sixth, father of the present Elizabeth the Second an English oak planted by Audrey Wurdemann Auslander, great great granddaughter of Percy Bysshe Shelley. In 1941, Alfred Noyes, author of the popular poem, "The Highwayman," Viscount Halifax, British Ambassador to the United States, and Sir Philip Gibbs, British journalist, all planted oaks here in the Shakespeare Garden.

On the memorable Sunday afternoon of September 1, 1935, the Sir Edward Elgar Chapter of the Daughters of the British Empire, under the direction of Mrs. Vera Newstead Rowley, held a meeting in the Shakespeare Garden. Garden lovers from all over the city were invited to a tour of the Gardens. A program of Morris dancing by literature students of Cleveland

College, excerpts from Shakespeares plays, and biographical sketches by members of the Lakewood Little Theatre Guild were presented.

David Belasco in the Shakespeare Garden

On May 28, 1948, the Royal Oak sapling grown from the 1937 Coronation seedling was planted by Cornelia Otis Skinner, who, on a visit to Cleveland, had expressed a desire to see the tree planted in the Shakespeare Garden by her famous father, Otis Skinner.

In July of 1951 the 25th anniversary of the Cultural Gardens was celebrated with a public, conducted tour of the Garden chain. Guests included many out-of-town members then attending the National Library Association convention, being held in Cleveland at that time. Also, a boulder was unveiled by Dr. Luther Evans, Librarian of Congress of Washington, D.C., in the Forest of Arden section of the Shakespeare Garden, bearing a passage from "As You Like It":

> "Books in Running Brooks,
>
> Sermons in Stones,
>
> And Good in Everything."

The Shakespeare Garden was laid out during the mayoralty term of Harry L. Davis, and while Alex Bernstein was director of city parks. Floyd Waite and Harry Hyatt, as park director and city forester respectively, succeeded them in this service. Considerable expansion took place during the administration of City Manager William R. Hopkins, when Frank S. Harmon was park director and Arthur L. Munson was city forester. Features added at this period included a rock garden background for the Shakespeare bust, the setting out of the Birnam Wood grove, and the extension of the garden area to the Bruot gateway. The active personal support given by City Manager Hopkins to the entire Garden project cannot be overestimated. Councilman J. E. Smith gave it energetic support at its outset, and served as committee chairman of the tercentenary event. Glenville High School also gave active backing.

"Englands sea wall has not confined his restless vision," wrote Leo Weidenthal of his favorite poet in his book, "From Diss Waggon," "Shakespeare as gardener sings the loftiest strain."

The dedication of the Shakespeare Garden was auspicious, for it proved to be the seedling from which was to spring the flourishing garland of the Cleveland Cultural Gardens.

Czech Cultural Garden
City of Cleveland Photograph

Czech Cultural Garden

In the Czech Cultural Garden are depicted the arts of the Bohemian, Moravian, and Silesian peoples. Dedicated in 1935, it is located on the upper East Boulevard drive, about 150 yards south of the intersection of the boulevard with St. Clair Avenue, its west boundary extending down to the lower East Boulevard drive. A circular lawn bordered by hedges and flanked by rose beds was designed by landscape architects, B. Ashburton Tripp and Maurice Cornell.

Forming the top border of a monumental stone wall is a sculptured frieze portraying the discovery of Bohemia and the American migration of the Czech people, bearing their rich cultural gifts. Surmounting the wall and facing the lawn is a series of four bronze heroic busts of celebrated Czech personages. These are Bedrich Smetana (1824-1884), composer of the popular comic opera, "The Bartered Bride" Dr. Miroslav Tyrs (1832-1884), educator and organizer of Sokol gymnastic societies Jan E. Purkyne (1787-1869), physiologist and Bozena Nemcova (1820-1862), woman novelist, famous for her book, "Babicka" (Little Grandmother).

Other busts in the Czech Garden have been raised to Frantisek Palacky (1798-1876), historian and statesman, and author of a "History of Bohemia" Anton Dvorak (1841-1904), world-renown composer whose impressions of America are portrayed in his beloved "New World Symphony" the Reverend Jendrich Simon Baar (1869-1929), priest and novelist and Karl Havlicek (1821-1856), publicist and journalist, who suffered imprisonment because of his fearless expression of patriotism and liberal views.

All the busts in the Czech Garden, as well as the wall frieze, are the work of Frank L. Jirouch, Cleveland-born sculptor of Czech descent.

Czech Garden activity has been notably vigorous since 1929, when a committee composed of Mrs. Marie Zeman, the Reverend Oldrich Zlamal, and Joseph Nemastil was formed, with Mr. Edward Kovanda as president, and Mrs. Roberta Manak as treasurer. On January 31, 1935, an exhibit of Czech art objects, arranged by Mrs. Manak, was held at the Higbee company, by which means funds were obtained and interest stimulate in the Czech Garden project. Czech lodges and Czech Catholic parishes were contacted and plans were drawn up by Frank Jirouch, Edward Kovanda, and Frank Vlchek for the setting out of trees, shrubbery, and monuments in a garden to cover about an acre of ground in the Cultural Garden chain.

Smetana

A permanent Czech Garden organization was formed soon after, with Edward Koster, Fred Holub, John Babka, Dr. E. Zeleznik, the Reverend V. Louzecky, and Alfred A. Benesch augmenting the previously formed committee. Permanent officers, elected during 1936, were E. C. Koster, president; Fred Holub, Bernard Plent, and Vaclav Frcka, vice-presidents; Marie A. Ruzicka, secretary; Marie Zemen, assistant secretary; Rose Dvorak, financial secretary; and Rose Triska, treasurer.

A three-year period of fund-raising card parties and social affairs enabled the group to proceed with the building of the garden proper. Many efforts, together with Federal and City aid, and the donations of statues by prominent Cleveland Czechs, enabled the treasury to complete the garden.

The Purkyne bust was donated by Victor Ptak, the Tyrs bust by Sokols Tyrs, the Dvorak bust by Frank C. Manak, the Palacky bust by a group of Cleveland Catholic clergy, the Smetana bust by Thomas L. Sidlo, and the Nemcova, bust by Mrs. Edward Nosek.

Frank Manak served as president from 1928 to 1940, and Herbert Zdara from 1941 to 1949, when the Tyrs, Nemcova, and Purkyne busts were placed and dedicated. Frank Bubna, at the present writing, is president.

President Benes of Czechoslovakia and Mayor Burton

The Czech Cultural Garden plot was dedicated on Sunday, October 6, 1935. Ceremonies began with the singing of the Star Spangled Banner. Officers of the Cultural Gardens League were presented to the assembled crowd. Addresses were delivered by William R. Hopkins, Harry L. Davis, then Mayor of Cleveland, Dr. Jaroslav Gardavsky, Czechoslovak Consul of Cleveland, and Professor Frank Bican. Musical selections were rendered by the Lumir-Hlahol and Vojan Singing Societies. Marie Zeman, Marie Ruzicka, and Monsignor Zlamal collaborated on a number of the program entitled "The Czech Cultural Garden", and the trees in the garden were decorated with fillets designed and donated by Miss Tonca Janovska of Praha.

On April 1, 1939, two linden trees from Bohemia were planted in the Czech Garden by President and Madam Benes of Czechoslovakia. This event typified the transplanting to the new world of the ideals of freedom and the rich culture of the Czech people, who first came to America as early as 1648, and gave us, in William Paca, a signer of the Declaration of Independence. Moravian missionaries did much to protect the early Colonists by teaching peace and faith to the Indians.

In 1786, ten years before the arrival at the Cuyahoga, of Moses Cleaveland and his surveyors, Moravian missionaries were building a settlement in the Cuyahoga Valley at the junction of the river and Tinkers Creek. Headed by Zeisberger and Heckewelder the group reared a number of log cabins and a chapel, and bestowed the name "Pilgeruh" or Pilgrims Rest upon the tiny settlement. Owing to the hostility of the Indians the venture did not prove successful and in time practically every trace of the buildings vanished.

From 1845 to the First World War, countless Czech immigrants enriched Americas farmlands and cities with their courage and industry. To the nobility alike of their labor and aspirations, the Czech Cultural Garden is dedicated as a memorial.

Reverend Baar

German Cultural Garden
City of Cleveland Photograph

German Cultural Garden

The German Cultural Garden, third in historical order in the chain, extends from the upper to the lower levels of East Boulevard. With its fountain and stone walks and double lateral sections of linden alleys, it centers about an impressive bronze two-figure statue of Johann Wolfgang Goethe (1749-1832) and Friedrich von Schiller (1759-1805), Germanys greatest two poet-philosophers. It is a replica of the famous Weimar statue, modeled in 1856 by Ernest Reitschal, the Dresden sculptor. Here tower the two mighty figures, joined in friendship as they were in life, and grandly dominate the spacious and imposing German Garden. The garden is entered at the upper Boulevard level through a triple-arched ornamental iron gate.

At the far end of the left lateral section is a bronze bust, a replica of the bust in Leipzig, modeled by Seffner, of Gotthold Ephraim Lessing (1729-1781), German critic and dramatist. At the far end of the right lateral section is a bronze bust of Heinrich Heine (1797-1856), world-famous poet and journalist of German birth. It is the work of K. Harald Isenstein of Berlin. The lower Boulevard section of the German Garden features a bust of Friedrich Jahn, founder of the first German turnverein program and originator of calisthenics.

The rare Unterburg marble fountain, dedicated in 1932, is a memorial to Friedrich Froebel, founder of the kindergarten system it once stood in the garden of the Archbishop of Salzburg, in Austria. More than one hundred varieties of shrubs, hedges, and trees imported from Germany decorate the German Garden, which was designed by Architect Herman Dercum. The linden trees were the gift of Mrs. John Spenzer, in memory of her husband, Dr. John Spenzer.

The German Cultural Garden Association was formed on July 26, 1929, at a meeting at the Socialer Turn Hall. On September 9, 1929, permanent officers were elected as follows: Miss Elsie Weitz, president; Charles Wolfram, secretary; and Albert Eisele, treasurer. Presidents of the Association serving through the years have been, in addition to Miss Weitz, Mrs. L. Schlather, Dr. Hugo Polt (professor at Western Reserve University), and Reverend Walter Klein, Minister of the Evangelical Reformed Church. Moving spirits and loyal members in the German Garden movement have been Mr. Charles Wolfram, founder and for many years president of the Cleveland Cultural Gardens Federation; Mrs. Rose Raeder, at the present writing financial secretary; William H. Engelmann, recording secretary; Mrs. Gertrude Benson, vice-president; Mr. and Mrs. Engelmann, founders, charter members, and trustees;

Miss Hedwig Wagner, Mr. Eisele, Mr. Dercum, Dr. Spenzer, Mr. Krueck, and Mr. and Mrs. Brenne served as early trustees. Maps and models for the projected garden were made and donated by Fred Mattmueller. The development of the German Garden was promoted in cooperation with the Park Department of the City of Cleveland. Funds were raised by a series of card parties, poetry readings, song recitals, and "coffee and cake" benefits. The Jahn bust was donated by the Socialer Turn Verein and Germania Vorwaerts Turn Verein. Since 1932 a group of women members of the German Cultural Garden Association has been active in the garden management.

The German Cultural Garden was dedicated on June 2, 1929, as part of a week-long celebration commemorating the Lessing-Mendelssohn Bicentennial. The Lessing bust was unveiled at this time, and the Goethe-Schiller statue, which formerly had stood in Wade Park, was rededicated in its new place of honor in the German Garden.

Musical selections were rendered by the Glenville and East High School Bands and the Vereinigte Mannerchor of Cleveland. The opening address was by William R. Hopkins, City Manager of Cleveland. The Lessing bust was presented to the city by Mrs. L. Schlather, chairman, and Miss Elsie Weitz, associate chairman of the Permanent Memorials Committee. The bust was accepted on behalf of the city by Mayor John Marshall. Professor R. W. Deering of Western Reserve University delivered the address on Lessing. Rabbi Abba Hillel Silver delivered the address on Moses Mendelssohn. The Star Spangled Banner was then played by the Consolidated Bands, while the American flag was unfurled, and a wreath was placed on the Lessing bust by Mr. David Jankau. The assemblage then marched to the Hebrew Garden, where a wreath was placed on the Moses Mendelssohn tablet by Mr. Ernest Mueller.

It was fitting that the bi-centennial tribute to these two great men who inspired and befriended each other in life, should have been jointly celebrated. Moses Mendelssohn, scholar and philosopher, was the prototype for Lessings stirring drama, "Nathan the Wise."

Miss Elsie Weitz and Mrs. Leonard Schlather at Dedication of Heine Bust

The Lessing-Mendelssohn Bi-centennial Commission consisted of William R. Hopkins, honorary chairman; Carl D. Friebolin, general chairman; Leo Weidenthal and Charles J. Wolfram, vice chairmen; Carl Raid, treasurer. Charles Wolfram served as chairman of the executive committee; Mrs. L. Schlather and Miss Elsie Weitz as chairman and associate chairman, respectively, of the Committee on Permanent Memorials. Samuel Newman was chairman of the Park Celebration Committee; Lewis Drucker, director of publicity; Edward J. Schweid, general secretary; Dr. E. B. De Sauze and A. H. Friedland, chairman and associate chairman respectively of the School Committee; Mrs.

Jennie K. Zwick, chairman of the Speakers Committee; Linda A. Eastman, chairman of the Library Committee; and Conrad Krueck and Charles De Harrack, chairman and associate chairman respectively of the Music Committee. Carl D. Friebolin was chairman of the German Garden dedication program.

A long list of enthusiastic members and sponsors also contributed to the inspiring success of the Cleveland Lessing-Mendelssohn Bi-centennial, which was dedicated in the spirit of the men it honored to good will and tolerance. Because of the significance of its German Cultural Garden undertaking, the Lessing-Mendelssohn Bi-centennial Commission was chosen by the Charles Eisenman Award Committee to receive the Eisenman Award for 1929. The award of $500 was contributed for the further development of the German Garden.

Lessing

The Father Jahn bust was dedicated on May 1, 1931.

The Heine bust was unveiled and presented to the City of Cleveland by William R. Hopkins and accepted by Mayor John D. Marshall, on June 14th, 1931, on the 75th anniversary of the death of the poet. Musical setting of Heines poems were rendered by the Cleveland Vereinigte Saenger. Principal addresses were by Professor Ernst Feise, of Johns Hopkins University, and Rabbi Barnett R. Brickner of the Euclid Avenue Temple. The ceremony concluded with the singing of America by all present. The sponsoring executive committee of the Heine Memorial Commission consisted of William R. Hopkins, chairman; Dr. Robert E. Vinson, Miss Linda A. Eastman and R. G. Jones, vice chairmen; Carl Raid, treasurer; Jennie K. Zwick, secretary; and Carl D. Friebolin, Alfred A. Benesch, Miss Elsie Weitz, Leo Weidenthal, Charles J. Wolfram, Charles De Harrack, C. R. Brenne, Albert Eisele, Professor E. B. De Sauze, Max E. Meisel, Fred G. Folberth, Miss Mildred Chadsey, and Clarence S. Metcalf.

Mme. Schumann-Heink

Guests of honor who have planted trees in the German Garden have included Graf Von Luckner, on April 21, 1931, and Madame Schumann-Heink, on September 7, 1933.

The purpose of the German Cultural Garden Association as set forth in Article II of its constitution, was to "awaken by honest and broad study, investigation and promulgation of the underlying principles of German Literature, Art, Science, and Culture, past and present, and thereby exemplify and emphasize their cultural value as contributions to mankind."

The aims of the Association, thus stated, have been generously fulfilled.

Greek Cultural Garden
City of Cleveland Photograph

Greek Cultural Garden

The Greek Cultural Garden is a sunken garden following the lines of a Greek cross. Its simple, classical effect, bridging the gap in spirit between the Periclean age and the modern age it most resembles --the American--is obtained without flowers.

The entrance is guarded by two Doric columns which are replicas of the ones a visitor sees while viewing the Parthenon on the Acropolis in Athens, Greece and opens on a westerly vista terminating in a reflecting pool and circular seats. Terraces formed of square-cut sandstone are planted with ilex, coloneastus, myrtle, and sweetbay, with cedars and Lombardy poplars to give the spire-like impression of cypresses. Maurice Cornell was garden architect.

The chief feature of this garden is a pylon symbolizing the wall of the Parthenon, dedicated to the Greek spirit in philosophy, art, literature, and science. It is inscribed with the names of Solon, Ictinus, Callicrates, Phidias, Aristophanes, Pericles, Euripides, Sophocles, Aeschylus, Homer, Praxiteles, Zeuxis, Apelles, Myron, Lysippus, Scopas, Sappho, Socrates, Anaxagoras, Aristotle, Plato, Aristarchus, Demosthenes, Pindar, Archimedes, Herodotus, Xenophon, Thucydides, Euclid, Hippocrates, Ptolemy, Pythagoras, Polycletus, and El Greco.

The ancient Greek architects devoted themselves above all to the problems of the column and lintel and the creation of beautiful temples. The open-air life which the climate invited, the simplicity of Greek ideals and respect for tradition, all favored the creation of forms of architecture which no later Western people has even forgotten.

It is in Greece that the personality of individual architects first became clear. The development of architecture was in extreme refinement, unity, beauty, symmetry and in musical harmony with physical laws.

This stately garden, with its serenity and dignity, is a fitting symbol of the great ideas it represents. For it is a sanctuary to the ancient Greek spirit of the search for truth and the supreme conquest of beauty.

The Greek Garden was officially dedicated on June 2, 1940, with James C. Mylonas as program chairman. Kimon Diamantopoulos, minister of Greece to the United States cut a blue and white ribbon stretched between the two Doric columns at the entrance, this formally opening the garden. Archbishop Athenagoras of New York, head of the Greek Orthodox

Church in North and South America, blessed the garden and was the central figure in a picturesque procession later in the program.

Dr. Elie George, president of the Greek Cultural Garden Association presented the garden to Cleveland with words: "May we and our children enjoy it and keep in our hearts the principles of cooperation which have made this garden possible." Mayor Harold H. Burton, in accepting the garden on behalf of the city, hailed two outstanding traits in the Greek character: simplicity and a perfect sense of proportion. Principal speaker was Governor Lausche, at the time Common Pleas Judge. "We must join hands in giving strength and faith to the government of the United States," he said. "It is only in the kind of spirit exhibited here today that we can carry on the true ideals of our government. Each race gives something to America. And all of us together will make a greater, better and permanent America." The choir of the Greek Orthodox Church of the Annunciation sang Greek and American anthems.

Funds for the Greek Garden were initially raised in 1938 by the Hellenic clubs of Cleveland, which organized to defray the cost through a series of lectures and other events.

On August 14, 1949, on the 125th anniversary of the death of Lord Byron, an evergreen tree was dedicated to his memory in the Greek Cultural Garden thus adding Cleveland as an abiding place of the poets liberty-loving spirit, to Missolonghi, where his heart is buried and to England, where are enshrined his other mortal remains. Major Edward J. Hobbs, British Consul in Cleveland, gave the chief address, sketching Byrons stormy career, and paying tribute to this proud, sensitive, and courageous hero. The evergreen was dedicated with the unfurling of a broad blue and white ribbon--the Greek national colors--from around the tree. As part of the ceremony, five young ladies danced the Kalamatiano, an old Greek folk dance. Miss Mary E. Hoover, librarian of the Cleveland Public Library, Euclid-East 101st Street Branch read from Byrons poem, "Don Juan," these lines of haunting beauty:

> "The mountains look on Marathon--
>
> And Marathon looks on the sea
>
> And musing there an hour alone,
>
> I dreamed that Greece might still be free
>
> For standing on the Persians grave,
>
> I could not deem myself a slave."

Honored guests included Menelaos Chopis, acting Greek Consul from Chicago, Judges Julius Kovachy and Joseph Artl, Charles J. Wolfram, then president of the Cleveland Cultural Gardens Federation, and representatives from the Hellenic, British, and Scottish Societies. Congratulations were offered to the Greek community of Cleveland on the Byron memorial by Ralph S. Locher, secretary to Governor Frank J. Lausche, by Emil Bartunek, secretary to Mayor Thomas A. Burke, and by Charles J. Wolfram. The event was under the auspices of the Womens Auxiliary of the Laconian Society, and George N. Kalkas, president of the Laconian Society was mast of ceremonies. The dedication concluded with a tour of the Cleveland Cultural Gardens.

Pioneers in Greek Garden activity were Philip D. Peppas, V. John Harris, Nick Copanos, Gus Passalis, George N. Kalkas, James C. Mylonas, and Dr. Elie George, Reverend Chrysogomos Lavriotis, A. G. Panagotoulos, Harry Collins, Louis Pappas, Mosky Moskos, Constantine Vilos, Theodore Bibicos, Michael Johanides, Louis Pappas, Spiros Stratis, and Antonios Chiotes.

View of the Greek Cultural Garden-Looking East

Plans for the future development of the Greek Cultural Garden have included the portrayal of renowned leaders in Greek thought and culture who moulded the course of civilization. Among them:

Socrates (469-399 B.C.), Greek philosopher, who devoted himself to the education of youth, believing that he was called to strive, by means of his teaching in the Agora, for a revival of moral feeling and the creation of a scientific foundation for truth and moral principles and who held that virtue is capable of being taught, that it brings one closest to Divine perfection and that all wickedness stems from ignorance;

Plato (427-347 B.C.), disciple of Socrates, whose philosophy stresses the teaching that reality belongs not to the individual thing, but to the general idea that individual things are fleeting copies of the form or idea, which dwells in the changeless unity forever, and is the sole purpose of real knowledge that linked with the theory of ideas is the doctrine of reminiscence or recollection, which contends that the soul has beheld the ideas in a previous stage of existence;

Aristotle (384-321 B.C.), famed scientific investigator and first philosophical writer to make a strict separation of the branches of philosophy, dividing them into logic, metaphysics, physics, ethics, politics and the philosophy of art tutor of Alexander, the son of Philip of Macedonia and the future world conqueror founder in Athens of the school at the Lyceum where he taught and directed scientific experiments during the closing years of his life.

The Byron Tree Near the Foot of North Entrance Steps

These and other leaders in the realm of philosophy and culture made the small nation of Greece a mighty influence in the shaping of the course of civilization. The thoughts of her sages, artists and dreamers moulded the thinking of myriads who followed them and her courageous struggles to regain her liberty were supported by inspired writers and thinkers of the modern age, who like Byron believed that it was the duty of lovers of democracy to support her cause.

Today, the mountains of Greece still look on Marathon and Marathon looks on a sea that laves the shores of a land whose people, heirs to a mighty culture, dwell in peace and in freedom.

Hebrew Cultural Garden
City of Cleveland Photograph

Hebrew Cultural Garden

First to be established under the new conception of a chain of gardens was the Hebrew Cultural Garden, the site for which was dedicated in 1926.

Located across the roadway and just southwest of the Shakespeare Garden, it is an oriental garden in three sections in a circular forest-tree setting. The stone walks are laid out to form the chief-motif--the six-pointed Star, or Shield, of David.

A hexagonal pool in the center reflects a pink Georgia marble fountain, its seven slender columns representing the seven Pillars of Wisdom, and inscribed with the quotation, in Hebrew characters, from Solomons Book of Proverbs:

"Wisdom hath built herself a house she hath hewn her out seven pillars."

The garden was designed by Landscape Architect T. Ashburton Tripp.

At four points of the Star of David are bronze portrait reliefs of world renowned philosophers. Moses Maimonides, Biblical scholar and physician, was born in Cordova, Spain, in 1135 and died in Cairo, Egypt, in 1204. Baruch Spinoza (1632-1677), Spanish-born philosopher of Amsterdam, was a major, dynamic force in the development of Western civilization and moulder of the thoughts of such great figures as Lessing, Goethe, and Coleridge. Moses Mendelssohn (1729-1786), grandfather of the composer, represents a modern school of Jewish thought, and translated the Bible into German. Achad Haam (pseudonym of Asher Ginsburg, 1856-1927) was the leader of cultural Zionism and a great writer who was responsible for the revival of the Hebrew language. The olive tree, the tree most characteristic of Hebrew history, figures prominently in the planting of the Philosophers Circle.

A smaller, adjoining garden on the left, the "music section", is planted in the shape of a Hebrew harp, or lyre. It was dedicated in July of 1937 with the unveiling of a monument bearing one plaque of three portrait heads of Jewish composers. These are Jacques Halevy (1799-1862), teacher of Gounod and Bizet, and composer of the opera, The Jewess Giacomo Meyerbeer (1791-1864), who wrote LAfricana, Les Hugenots, and Le Prophete and Karl Goldmark (1830-1915), author of Queen of Sheba, and uncle of the wife of former Chief Justice Louis Brandeis. Funds for this plaque were provided by the Gan Ivri Womens League.

*Mrs. Jennie K. Zwick, Rabbi Abba Hillel Silver,
Dr. Chaim Weizmann, City Manager Hopkins,
Leo Weidenthal*

To the right of the main section is the Poets Corner, a ravine rock garden containing Palestinian plants and bronze tablets with appropriate inscriptions from Hebrew literature. This completes the general design of the Hebrew Garden. A dominating feature of the rock garden is a large boulder, set with a circular plaque, a bronze bas-relief, to the memory of Rebecca Gratz of Philadelphia. She was the founder of the first Jewish religious school in America, and is famous as the prototype of Rebecca, the heroine of Scotts Ivanhoe. She lived from 1781 to 1869. The Gratz plaque is flanked by plaques of Henrietta Szold and Emma Lazarus.

The dedication of the Hebrew Garden site occurred during an important event: the visit of Chaim Nachman Bialik to Cleveland. Acclaimed as the greatest Hebrew poet since the Prophet Isaiah, Bialik had come from Palestine on an American tour in the cause of Zionism. On May 5, 1926, in the presence of a large crowd despite steady rainfall, Bialik planted three Cedars of Lebanon in the future Poets Corner of the Hebrew Garden, and delivered an eloquent address in Hebrew, translated by the late Rabbi Solomon Goldman. City Manager William R. Hopkins, in his speech of greeting, paid tribute to the contributions of Hebrew writers to world culture. Edmund Vance Cooke, Cleveland poet, Councilman A. R. Hatton, and A. H. Friedland, superintendent of Clevelands Hebrew schools, also participated.

Maimonides

In his address, Bialik, Hebrew translator of Shakespeares "Julius Caesar," emphasized the joint literary domination of Shakespeare and the Hebrew Bible in modern culture, noting at the same time that the Hebrew Garden site faced the Shakespeare Garden.

"Today Chaim Bialik plants the older poetry into a newer earth," said Mr. Cooke, referring to the Cedars of Lebanon, "immortal in a truer sense than material reality, immortal in song, and story...the symbolism of their evergreen fragrance representing an ancient faith." Mr. Cooke concluded his address with the words, "And the significance of it all is that this ceremony occurs not in hoary Palestine, or in dreamy Stratford-on-Avon, but in this modern, throbbing, vital City of Cleveland, unsurpassed in its modernity by any city in the world."

In memory of Julius Schweid, Cleveland civic and Jewish communal leader, a plaque of Israels renowned poet, Chaim Nachman Bialik was dedicated in the Hebrew Garden on July 25, 1954, more than 28 years after Bialiks visit to the site of the garden. The plaque, designed by Dr. Bernard Cooper, was the gift of a sponsoring committee of which Edward J. Schweid and Dr. Haskell H. Schweid, sons of Julius Schweid, were members.

The formal opening of the Philosophers Circle of the Hebrew Garden, October 30, 1927, was a national event. Ceremonies were participated in by noted Jews from all parts of the world, by civic leaders, and by rabbis of Cleveland. Speakers included Dr. Judah L. Magnes, chancellor of the Hebrew University in Jerusalem, Henrietta Szold, founder of Hadassah, Rabbi Barnett R. Brickner, Rabbi Solomon Goldman, Rabbi Abba Hillel Silver, and Rabbi Abraham Nowak, of Cleveland. Miss Szold and Rabbi Magnes planted cedars at the Achad Haam plaque. Rabbi Brickner unveiled the Mendelssohn plaque, a gift of the Gan Ivri Womens League. Rabbi Silver unveiled the Achad Haam plaque, given by the Cleveland Zionist District and Cleveland Hebrew schools Rabbi Goldman unveiled the Maimonides plaque, memorial gift made to the garden by Mrs. Rae Roodman.

Henrietta Szold

The Spinoza plaque, gift of the Cleveland Lodge of Bnai Brith had previously been unveiled with impressive ceremony to mark the 250th anniversary of the philosophers death. A. H. Friedland, noted Cleveland poet and educator, delivered the principal address.

Both the Gratz monument and the rock garden were dedicated in September, 1932, as part of the Sir Walter Scott centennial celebration. Park Commissioner John Brown accepted the memorial for the city. Max E. Meisel delivered the address on Rebecca Gratz. Mrs. Jennie K. Zwick made the presentation of the plaque, a gift of the Gan Ivri League. Dr. William Auld of Elyria gave the address on Sir Walter Scott.

Completing a grouping of memorials to famous Jewish women in this section are bronze plaques of Henrietta Szold and Emma Lazarus. The Henrietta

Szold plaque was dedicated June 4, 1950, the 90th anniversary of her birth. She was founder of Hadassah and creator of the Youth Aliyah. The plaque was a gift of the Cleveland Chapter of Hadassah.

Mrs. Albert P. Schoolman of New York, member of the Hadassah National Board, spoke on Henrietta Szold. Greetings were by Albert A. Woldman, director of Ohio Industrial Relations Department. Mrs. Lewis W. Phillips was chairman of the Henrietta Szold Committee.

Balik

The Emma Lazarus plaque was dedicated June 16, 1949, to mark the 100th anniversary of her birth. The Federation of Jewish Womens Organizations, presented the plaque, which is inscribed with a phrase from the sonnet of Emma Lazarus which is affixed in bronze to the pedestal of the Statue of Liberty:

"Give me your tired, your poor,

Your huddled masses yearning to breathe free,

The wretched refuse of your teeming shore.

Send these, the homeless, tempest-tost to me,

I lift my lamp beside the golden door."

These words reflect the spirit of the Cultural Gardens, which symbolically, also "lifts its lamp beside the golden door."

To the right of the Philosophers Circle and at the entrance to the rock garden is a bronze memorial plaque of Milton B. Schweid. The tablet is inscribed with a quotation from Ecclesiasticus, concluding with the following lines:

"Bountifulness is as a garden of abundance. And benevolence endureth forever."

Also in this section is a boulder to which is affixed a plaque inscribed with a passage from the writings of Emma Lazarus:

"The Soul at Peace Reflects the Peace Without. Forgetting Grief as Sunset Skies Forget the Mornings Transient Shower." The boulder was presented to the Hebrew Garden by Cleveland Bnai Brith Auxiliary, Cleveland Heights Bnai Brith Auxiliary, and Balfour Bnai Brith Auxiliary, honoring the Womens Grand Lodge District No. 2 Bnai Brith.

Dr. Chaim Weizmann, who in 1949 became Israels first president, in 1927 visited the Garden and planted several Cedars of Lebanon. This planting was sponsored by the Keren Hayesod Womens Club. The Gan Ivri Womens League took part in this event.

In 1937 Cleveland Jewry celebrated the 100th anniversary of its existence in the community, with a Hebrew Garden festivity tree planting program. Descendants of Simson Thorman, Clevelands first Jewish settler, participated.

Set in a semi-circular niche just beyond the fountain and opposite the entrance to the Hebrew Garden is a bronze memorial plaque dedicated to the memory of Max E. Meisel by his Bnai Brith associates.

Reliefs and plaques in the Hebrew Garden are the work of Cleveland artists of renown. The Musicians and Gratz plaques are by Miriam E. Cramer, the Spinoza portrait by Max Kalish, the Szold plaque by Esther Samolar, the Emma Lazarus head by Walter Sinz. The three remaining philosophers plaques are the work of Alexander Blazys.

Active in the establishment of the Hebrew Garden were Leo Weidenthal and Mrs. Jennie K. Zwick. Mr. Weidenthal, editor of the Jewish Independent, in 1936 received the Eisenman award of $1,000 for distinguished citizenship. Immediately upon the citation, Mr. Weidenthal turned over the $1,000 as a contribution toward the completion of the Hebrew Garden.

It was on March 5, 1927, that the Gan Ivri Womens League was organized at the home of Mrs. Jennie K. Zwick, for the purpose of developing the Hebrew Cultural Garden. At this meeting, plans were made for the planting of Cedars of Lebanon in the garden by Dr. Chaim Weizmann, then president of the World Zionist Organization, who was soon to visit Cleveland. Officers elected at this meeting were Mrs. Zwick, president; Mrs. Henry Frankel, treasurer; Mrs. O. Fink and Mrs. O. K. Greenberg, financial secretaries; Mrs. L. Dembo, recording secretary; Mrs. L. W. Phillips, publicity secretary.

On March 9, a committee representing the organization, called upon City Manager William R. Hopkins and presented plans for the embellishment and development of the garden. The committee consisted of Mrs. Zwick, Mrs. B. R. Brickner, Mrs. Henry Frankel, Mrs. L. W. Klusner, Mrs. D. Gara, Mrs. O. K. Greenberg, and Mrs. L. W. Phillips. The meeting was attended by Sculptor Max Kalish and Leo Weidenthal.

On Monday, April 11, Councilman Abner H. Goldman introduced an ordinance establishing the Cultural Garden and defining its units. The site chosen was diagonally across from the Shakespeare Garden, on the upper East Boulevard.

Among other pioneers in the Hebrew Garden cause were Edward J. Schweid, the late A. H. Friedland, the late Max E. Meisel, and the late Judge Lewis Drucker.

Present officers in the Hebrew Garden Association are Leo Weidenthal, president; Edward J. Schweid, vice-president; and Mrs. L. W. Phillips, secretary-treasurer.

The Hebrew Garden in its setting of tall old trees gleams "as a garden of abundance" reflecting teachings that have guided the way of myriads through the passing ages.

View of the Hebrew Garden from the Main Entrance

Hungarian Cultural Garden
City of Cleveland Photograph

Hungarian Cultural Garden

The Hungarian Cultural Garden is constructed on two levels along the upper boulevard, and overlooks lower East Boulevard. Designed by a well-known architect of Budapest, Hungary, it is a distinguished garden from the standpoint of compact, opulent, and formal landscape style. The entrance is through a delicately patterned wrought-iron gateway, the gift of the Verhovay Insurance Association. It is like the traditional type of archway leading to country estates in Hungary and is decorated with two small delightful peasant figures in bronze. In the principal plot on the upper level, a rectangular reflecting pool and fountain are set in a pattern of low walls and geometric walks of brick, stone, and marble, and rich plantings of the growths best known in Hungary--hawthorn, yew, cotoneasters, and azaleas. Two linden trees, formal flower beds, and brick, stone, and marble walls and walks are the features of the lower garden. Two wing sections, formal arrangements of lawn, brick paths, and sculptured stone benches, adjoin the larger upper garden. In the section to the left of the entrance is a bas-relief of Franz Liszt.

For the promotion of the Hungarian Cultural Garden project, a Cultural Garden Committee of the United Hungarian Societies of Cleveland had been formed with Louis Petrash as president and Nicholas F. Molnar as secretary. On September 24, 1934, the commission gave public notice of its initial venture in a statement opening as follows:

"The establishment of the Hungarian Cultural Garden is actively under way. A meeting will be held, Thursday evening, Oct. 4, 1934, at 8 oclock at the Hollenden Hotel Lounge, for the purpose of completing and enlarging the sponsor committee, together with making proper arrangements for the celebration of Liszt Week, commencing October 15, 1934, with the dedication exercises to be held, Sunday, October 21, 1934."

The United Societies then named a permanent commission consisting of Municipal Judge Louis Petrash, chairman; Nicholas F. Molnar, secretary; Attorney Stephen Kormendy, treasurer; Stephen Gobozy, George M. Kovachy, Albert Tudja and Emery Hoffer.

Madach

The site of the Hungarian Garden was dedicated on October 21, 1934, upon the occasion of the 123rd anniversary of the birth of Franz Liszt, with the unveiling of the bas-relief of the Hungarian composer.

In honoring Liszt, the Hungarian Cultural Garden leaders chose, at the outset, an Hungarian, whose name was destined to tower high in the history of music, as composer and as pianist. Son of Adam Liszt, the boy Liszt appeared in public at the age of nine with great success. His first appearance in concert in Vienna, was on December 1, 1822. Liszt appeared in London in his early youth and later became an outstanding figure in the great art and cultural center of Weimar. In 1859, he transferred his center of activity to Rome. His last appearance upon a concert of the Musical Society of Luxembourg. His death occurred on July 31 of that year.

The Liszt plaque is the Hungarian Cultural Garden is the work of John Tenkacs, Cleveland sculptor. Speakers at the dedication included: Dr. Louis Alexy,

Hungarian Consul; Joseph Remenyi, Mayor Harry L. Davis; former City Manager William R. Hopkins and Charles J. Wolfram, president of the Cultural Garden League.

The program was opened by Louis Petrash, chairman of the Cultural Garden Committee. Nicholas F. Molnar, secretary of the committee and secretary of the City Plan Commission of Cleveland, was master of ceremonies. Assistant Police Prosecutor Stephen Gobozy, president of the United Hungarian Societies delivered the welcoming address.

An ode to Liszt by Dr. Ladislaus Polya was recited by the author and a Liszt Rhapsody was played by the string ensemble of the Liszt Conservatory of Music.

The United Hungarian Societies in 1936 launched a campaign to raise funds for the Hungarian Cultural Garden.

The finance committee, headed by Municipal Judge Julius M. Kovachy, included Parks Director Hugo E. Varga, Dr. William Riegelhaupt, John Schreier, Dr. Stephen Ciprus, John Jakab, Peter Gerzsenyi, the Rev. Emery Tanos, the Rev. Stephen Porantunszky, Mrs. John Volosin, Mrs. Albert Kiraly, Louis Toth, Mrs. Amelia Doby, John B. Toth, Frank E. Boldizsar, Mrs. Esther Kay, Ignatz Fanchaly, Dr. John Kovacs, Stephen Kovacs, Dr. Nicholas Steiner, Erno Fedak, Emery Olexo, Elmer Kallay, Mrs. Carl Herczeg.

In 1937 an aggressive campaign was launched among Cleveland Hungarians for the raising of the $4,000 requisite for the completion of their garden. This was accomplished by church appeals, personal contributions, and benefit concerts of high artistic quality. The Hungarian Cultural Garden Association at that time was made up of Municipal Judge Julius

Kovachy, president; Dr. Stephen Ciprus, vice-president; Dr. John Majoros, secretary; and John Kish, treasurer. Members of the executive committee were Judge Louis Petrash, Louis Toth, John Jakab, Ignatz Fanchaly, Paul Nagy, Stephen Gobozy, and Stephen Kormendy.

The Hungarian Garden was officially and formally dedicated on July 10, 1938. A colorful parade of some 5,000 members of Hungarian organizations, many of them in native costumes, marched along lower East Boulevard to the speakers stand at the lower end of the Hungarian Garden, where a crowd of 20,000 persons awaited them. The combined Hungarian Singing Societies, a chorus of 300 mixed voices, directed by Carl Tomasi, sang several selections from their position on a tree-shrouded hillside overlooking the garden. Nicholas Roosevelt, former minister to Hungary, was the principal speaker. He appealed to Americans to preserve the intellectual and spiritual freedom which is assured by democratic and parliamentary government. Councilman Stephen Gobozy, president of the United Hungarian Societies, introduced the speakers. Municipal Judge Julius M. Kovachy, president of the Hungarian Cultural Garden-Association, officially presented the garden to the city. Mayor Harold H. Burton in accepting the gift, expressed the thanks of the people of the city, and praised the vital cultural interests of Cleveland Hungarians. United States Senator Robert J. Bulkey cited the role of the Works Progress Administration in Cultural Gardens history as one which could not be measured in merely monetary terms. Dr. Louis Alexy, Hungarian Consul General for the middle west, conveyed the thanks of the Hungarian government to the federal, state, and municipal agencies which aided in the construction of the garden. Other speakers included Joseph Fodor, prominent in Cleveland Hungarian affairs; Joseph Darago, Pittsburgh supreme president of the Verhovay Aid Society; William B. Pecsok, spokesman for Governor Martin L. Davey; Hugo E. Varga, city park director; Congressman Robert Crosser Emery Kiraly, supreme treasurer of the Reform Federation of America; Municipal Judge Louis Petrash, first president of the Hungarian Garden; Charles J. Wolfram, then president of the Cultural Garden League; and Stephen Ciprus, vice-president of the Hungarian Cultural Garden Association.

On September 7, 1941, a 40-foot steel flagpole and an American flag were dedicated in an impressive ceremony in the Hungarian Garden. The pole and its ornate base were the gift of the Magyar Club of Cleveland. The program opened with selections by the Buckeye Road Hungarian Baptist Church Band. Judge Julius M. Kovachy, president of the Hungarian Cultural Garden Association, presided.

On July 23, 1950, at the conclusion of the annual One World Day celebration, marking the 25th anniversary of the founding of the Cultural Gardens, a bronze statue of Imre Madach, philosophical dramatist and author of "The Tragedy of Man" was dedicated in the Hungarian Garden. Dr. Joseph Remenyi delivered the principal address on the works of Madach. The bust was the work of Sculptor Alexander Finta, and the dedication was jointly sponsored by the Hungarian Cultural Garden Association and the United Hungarian Societies of Cleveland.

Dedication of a memorial to another outstanding figure in world culture and in Hungarys great literary history took place on May 23, 1954, with the presentation to the Hungarians Cultural Garden of a bronze bust of the poet, Endre Ady (1877-1919). Ady, who has been referred to as a 20th century counterpart of Petofi was extolled by speakers at a program in the section of the Hungarian Garden designed for busts of noted writers and other leaders in Hungarys cultural life.

Ady

Master of ceremonies at the unveiling program was Judge Julius M. Kovachy. The National Anthem was sung by Mrs. Louis Bodnar. Rev. Gabor Brachna delivered the invocation. The dedication address was delivered by Dr. Frank Ujlaki and the unveiling address by Judge Kovachy, president of the Hungarian Cultural Garden Association. A greeting by Mayor Anthony J. Celebrezze followed and there were songs by St. Stephens Choir. The program also included songs by the Reformed Church Choir. Greetings from the United Hungarian Societies were extended by Andrew Dono. Leo Weidenthal, president of the Cultural Garden Federation also addressed the gathering and Judge Louis Petrash, vice president of the Federation extended the communitys greetings. A wreath was placed on the memorial by Frank Magyary in the name of the Rakoczi Society. Kalman Revesz, secretary of Verhovay also placed a wreath on the bust.

At the present writing, Appellate Judge Julius M. Kovachy is president of the Hungarian Cultural Garden Association, Mrs. Margaret Szabo and Miss Lily Volosin are vice-presidents, Stephen Gobozy is secretary, Joseph Szalay, is treasurer, and Municipal Judge Louis Petrash, Mr. and Mrs. Kalman Kolsvary, Carl Helwig, Andrew Dono, Mrs. Joseph Dunasky, Mathias Gallo, Mrs. Andrew Balazik, Steven Kovach, Charles Kautzky, John Marton, and Ferenz Simon, are directors. Executive officers and delegates to the Cultural Garden Federation are Judges Louis Petrash and Julius M. Kovachy, Miss Lily Volosin, and Stephen Gobozy.

Judge Louis Petrash, Miss Lily Volosin,
Judge Julius Kovachy, Miss Clara Lederer

Officers of former years have included, in addition to Judge Kovachy as president, Dr. Stephen Ciprus, vice-president, Dr. John Majoros, secretary, and John Kish, treasurer. Former directors have been, in addition to Judge Kovachy, Dr. Stephen Ciprus, John J. Kish, Judge Louis Petrash, Dr. John Majoros, Joseph Fodor, Stephen Bogozy, Louis Toth, John Jakab, Paul Nagy, Stephen Kormendy, and Ignatz Fanchaly.

A charming feature of Hungarian Garden history has been its annual Visitation Day celebration, marked by gypsy music, flag raising ceremonies, speeches by prominent Cleveland Hungarians, and the serving of Hungarian pastries and coffee with whipped cream to guests by members of Hungarian womens organizations in native costume.

Dr. Joseph Remenyi, professor of Comparative Literature at Western Reserve University, distinguished both as critic of international reputation and creative writer in his native Hungary, and for many years a dynamic cultural asset on the Cleveland scene, sums up for us the implied ethnic and individual significance of the Hungarian Cultural Garden. He points out that the Hungarians, a Finno-Ugric people with a thousand year old history on the European continent, speak a language which tends to isolate them from a complete understanding of their position in the progress of European civilization. "Hungary, for centuries the defender of Christendom against Ottoman invaders," Dr. Remenyi says, "was also the defender of her culture which developed parallel with that of the West. Scholasticism, the Renaissance, the Reformation, and Counter-Reformation, the Age of Enlightenment, have their corresponding periods in Hungarian history. Throughout the centuries political, cultural and religious leaders endeavored to co-ordinate western orientation with national loyalties." Dr. Remenyi cites the music of Bela Bartok, modern Hungarian composer, as a vital symbol of the Hungarian cultural spirit, insofar as it portrays "an interplay between the emotional and ethical forces of national traditions and those of individualism, as understood in Western Europe." Dr. Remenyi comments on the design of the Hungarian Cultural Garden by stating that it is in accordance with traditional aesthetic expressions, and that Cleveland Hungarians have not lost sight of their rural or artisan past. "The garden also displays the personal qualities of Hungarian culture," Dr. Remenyi says, "reflected in the tangible symbols of the plaque of Franz Liszt, whose compositions were influenced by folk tunes, and the bust of Imre Madach, the philosophical dramatist."

Liszt Plaque-Day of Dedication

Future plans for the adornment of the Hungarian Garden with busts honoring famous Hungarians who have contributed to both national Hungarian and to universal culture, included the commemoration of Sandor Petofi, greatest Hungarian lyrist, epic genius, and master of the Hungarian language Janos Arany, and memorials in honor of Mor Jokai, popular, romantic novelist Farkas Bolyai, mathematician Ignac

Semmelweis, medical genius Mihaly Munkacsy, world-renowned landscape and portrait artist, painter of historical subjects, including the famous "Milton Dictating Paradise Lost to his Daughters " and Bela Bartok, composer of operatic, choral, symphonic, vocal, violin and piano works, in whose last string quartets there has been discovered a close spiritual kinship with those of Beethoven.

No more fitting conclusion than these remarks of Dr. Remenyi could be chosen for this chapter on the Hungarian Garden. "The Hungarian Garden design should not be viewed as a superimposed ornamental improvement of the past, but a logical and harmonious expression of a nations collective and individual spirit, side by side with similar expression of other nations. Here is an example of how true values are preserved in an American city. It proves that America does not consider the divergent cultural horizons of other nations incompatible with the basic ideology of democracy on the contrary, their values are recognized in accordance with the Jeffersonian view of mans place and dignity in our society."

Mid Portion of the Hungarian Cultural Garden

Irish Cultural Garden

Irish Cultural Garden

The Irish Cultural Garden is located at the Superior Avenue entrance of the Rockefeller Park Garden chain, and was dedicated in 1939. Here the Celtic cross is developed in turf, slate, and sandstone walks, and sedum-filled lunettes. Irish juniper, yew and white lilac, hawthorn, lavender and wisteria have been planted, and shamrocks, cowslips, and Shannon roses form the borders. There are beds of Killarney roses, and of the "Last Rose of Summer" species. Along a cinder path descending to the Irish Garden are planted Irish blackthorn, used in the making of a shillelagh, or cudgel. This "greenest of the park gardens" as it has proudly been called, was designed by Donald Gray. Thomas J. McManamon volunteered his services as supervising construction engineer.

An initial dedication of the Irish Garden took place on the afternoon of Sunday, May 28th, 1933, the 154th anniversary of the birth of the celebrated Irish poet, Thomas Moore. The Reverend Doctor Edward A. Kirby of St. Cecilias Parish Church delivered the principal address before an audience of 2000. Congressman Martin L. Sweeney, as master of ceremonies, introduced Cultural Garden League officers, other nationality group leaders, and specifically Mrs. Mary K. Duffy, tireless Irish group leader, together with Miss Mary Ellen Murphy, with the Gardens beginnings to its triumphant culmination. Ray T. Miller, Mayor of Cleveland, and William J. Corrigan also spoke, paying tribute to Irelands cultural gifts to the world. Irish music was presented by the Parmadale Band and the Joyce Kilmer Gaelic-American Club Quartet.

This charming garden was realized through the efforts of the Irish Cultural Garden Association, which, under the presidency of James J. Murray, in January of 1939 raised the initial $1500 to be augmented by Federal and City funds to a requisite $45,000. The assisting committee included: (Clergy) Auxiliary Bishop James Am McFadden, Msgr. John P. Treacy, Msgr. Hagan, Reverend Michael Moriarty, Reverend Martin Gallagher; (Professional) Dr. J. S. Tierney, Dr. J. J. Kelley, Parker Fulton, William J. Corrigan, John J. OMalley, Councilman Thomas J. Gunning, William J. Donlon, Lewis Reidy; (Finance) John T. Feighan, William J. Murphy; (Business) Edwin D. Barry, Thomas A. Ryan; (Labor) Thomas A. Lenehan, Albert Dalton; (Postal) Postmaster Michael F. ODonnell, James L. Collins; (Judges) Common Pleas Judges Frandk J. Merrick and Frank S. Day, Municipal Judge Perry A. Frey, and Municipal Judge Lillian M. Westropp; (Municipal Court) Frank Kelly, Martin Kinsella; (Police)

Captains Edward J. Flanagan and John T. Fleming; (Fire) Battalion Chiefs Emmet H. Byrne and Thomas F. McManamon, Fire Secretary John F. Horan; (City Officials) License Commissioner Joseph E. Cassidy; (County Officials) County Commissioner Joseph F. Gorman, County Prosecutor Frank T. Cullitan, Assistant County Prosecutor James P. Hart, Sheriff Martin ODonnell, County Clerk John J. Busher, County Purchasing Agent Leslie Monroe, Deputy County Engineer James R. Devitt, Chief Deputy Recorder Edward J. Coleman; (Federal Offices) Owen Corcoran; (Organizations) Patrick Lynch, Dan W. Duffy.

Barry Day Celebraion

The Irish Garden was officially dedicated on October 29, 1939. Music was by the Parmadale Band, the fife and drum corps of the Sons and Daughters of Eire, and the West Side Irish-American Club. Under banners of orange, white and green, the Knights of Columbus in black and red garb, stood at attention. The Reverend Father Stephen Driscoll, assistant pastor of St. Thomas Aquinas Church, blessed the garden. Common Pleas Judge Frank J. Merrick served as chairman. Principal speaker was Mayor Maurice J. Tobin of Boston, who stressed the Irish contribution to American over a period of three centuries. Congressman Martin L. Sweeney praised the Irish of the Homeland, and Mary K. Duffy also spoke. Harold H. Burton, Mayor of Cleveland, formally presented the garden to the Irish Cultural Garden Association, and Mr. John J. OMalley, vice-president of the Association, accepted in behalf of President James J. Murray, absent because of illness. A sad note marking this otherwise gala occasion was a prayer offered by Msgr. John R. Hagan, diocesan director of parochial schools, for Thomas J. McManamon, the engineer who had given so generously of his services to the Irish Garden, and whose death had occurred the day before the dedication.

At the conclusion of the dedication ceremonies, James J. Murray, association president, ill at his home, was presented by garden officials with a gold watch in appreciation of his splendid work in making this dream of the Irish Garden come true.

At a banquet in Hotel Hollenden that evening, Postmaster Michael F. ODonnell was toastmaster, and Bishop James A McFadden and Mayor Tobin, of Boston, and Mayor Burton, of Cleveland, were speakers.

On Sunday, May 11, 1952, Mothers Day, in a simple ceremony at the Irish Cultural Garden, tribute was paid to Ernest R. Ball, composer of many Irish ballads, including "Mother Machree." Mrs. E. C. Ingram of Lakeside, Ohio, daughter of the composer, who was born, reared and educated in Cleveland, and who was a piano teacher here during the early period of his musical career, planted a mountain laurel shrub in her fathers memory. County Prosecutor Frank T. Cullitan, and Judge John V. Corrigan, then State Representative, briefly reviewed Balls career, terming him as much responsible for the observance of Mothers Day as any other single American. In charge of this ceremony was Mrs. Mary K. Duffy, president of the Irish Cultural Garden League.

On June 21, 1953, the Reverend Patrick Peyton, famed leader of the Rosary Crusade, planted an Irish juniper tree in the Irish Garden. Father Peyton, who has travelled the world over preaching that "families that pray together stay together," recited the Rosary and delivered a short talk before a statue of the Blessed Virgin, placed in the garden for the occasion.

An interesting annual observance which has high-lighted Irish Garden history has been the Barry Day celebration held on a September Sunday each year in honor of Commodore John Barry. Born in County Wexford, Ireland, in 1745, John Barry enthusiastically espoused the cause of American independence, offering his services to the Continental Congress and being placed in command of the Brig Lexington with which he successfully engaged in many encounters. By reason of his services to his country in its early days, he became known as the "Father of the American Navy."

Officers of the United States Navy have been principal speakers at the Barry Day celebrations through the years, and include Lieutenant R. J. Mullarkey, Commander E. W. McKinley, Commander John C. Grogan, Lieutenant Commander James M. Brogan, Admiral Daniel V. Gallery, Captain Thomas B. Dugan, Admiral Daniel V. Gallery, Jr., and Commander John Thomas McLaughlin.

In 1953, Mayor Thomas A. Burke designated by city proclamation, September 13th as Commodore John Barry Day. On that day the program included the posting of the Colors by the United States Navy, the singing of the Star Spangled Banner by Jack Nealings, and Irish music and dances by Belle Conway, Patrick A. Donovan, Tom McLaughlin, Jimmy Giblin, and Tommy Byrne. Nathaniel R. Howard, editor of the Cleveland News, spoke on his recent trip to Ireland, and presented the

Irish Garden with stones he brought from the home of Daniel OConnell, known as "the great emancipator of Ireland." Of Derrynane, in County Kerry, OConnell won restoration of Irish citizenship rights from the British Parliament in the 1840s. The stones were accepted gratefully as a permanent addition to the Irish Garden by Mrs. Mary K. Duffy, president of the Irish Cultural Garden League. Principal speaker was Lieutenant Commander R. G. OMaley, Naval Air Station, Akron, Ohio. The benediction was by the Reverend Peter F. McCafferty, Assistant Pastor of St. Josephs Church.

"Commodore Barrys example of selfless devotion to duty has been, and continues to be, an inspiration to sailors of every generation," Commander OMaley said, in part. "He lives today whenever Americans are risking and giving their lives in conflict with the enemies of freedom...There is a fine symbolism to be found in the fact that the last command of Commodore Barry was the Frigate of the United States. When the keel, frames and deck of his last ship rotted away, long after his flag of command was hauled down, he still continued to live in the keel and framework of his larger loyalty-the United States of America."

Municipal Judge Lillian M. Westropp was general Chairman of the 1953 program, Judge John V. Corrigan was master of ceremonies, and Mrs. Mary K. Duffy, president of the Irish Cultural Garden League, was in charge of the arrangements. Other League officials assisting included Miss Mary Ellen Murphy, secretary; Mrs. Jack Kelly, Mrs. Frank Damon, treasurer; Mrs. Anna Davis, Mr. and Mrs. Pat Lynch (Mr. Lynch serving as Barry Day chairman), Mrs. P. J. Maloney, Mrs. Thomas Sullivan, Mr. and Mrs. Michael Giblin, Mrs. Lou Schwartzenberg, Mrs. Patrick OBrien, and Judge Frank Merrick. The West Side Irish-American Club has also always given generous assistance. The Barry Day events are jointly sponsored by the Commodore Barry Club of Cleveland, and the Irish Cultural Garden League.

*Irish Garden Approach
from Upper Boulevard*

    The history of Commodore John Barry, adopted patron of the Irish Cultural Garden, is the story of many Irish leaders who emigrated to America and so loved and fought so valiantly for this land. In the words of William Bell Clark, "No American naval hero has deserved of posterity greater appreciation of his career and received less than John Barry." Barry was the first captain of the first warship named after the first land battle of the Revolution. He was the first to capture a British warship and was named the first commissioned officer of the

United States Navy.

In keeping with the spirit of the Barry Day celebrations and the Irish Garden are these words of Judge John V. Corrigan:

"The one principal fact that has been emphasized here is the debt which we owe all our American heroes--past, present, and future--the men who have fought and fight to preserve our freedom and our independence. The Lafayettes, the Pulaskis, the Von Steubens, the Stefaniks, and the Barrys, and all the rest have enabled us to prove to the world that all sons of men are children of God before Whom all men kneel as equals. In honoring commodore Barry we do, in fact, honor all great Americans. And on this memorial day we all can join in the prayer of the eloquent poet:

"And Thou, Oh God, of Whom we hold our country and our freedom fair,

Within Thy tender love enfold this Land for all Thy people care.

Uplift our hearts above our fortunes high, Let not the good we have make us forget

The better things that in Thy heavens lie!

Keep still, amid the fever and the fret of all this eager life our thought on Thee,

The hope, the strength, the God of all the free."

The Irish Garden was, in the words of the Reverend Doctor Edward A. Kirby, dedicated "to the glory of nature and of God, to the good of our fellow-citizens, and as a memorial to the Land of Flowers-Ireland."

Set like an emerald in the Cultural Gardens chain of gems, this exquisite little garden is a symbol of universal hope, that is typical of the courageous and cheerful people who gave it.

Italian Cultural Garden
City of Cleveland Photograph

Italian Cultural Garden

The Italian Cultural Garden is designed on two levels in formal landscape style grandly conceived in the spirit of the Italian Renaissance.

The chief features of the upper level garden are a large circular marble fountain, a stone parapet, and, terminating the right arm of its North-South axis, a bronze bust of the poet Virgil. Mounted on a stone column taken from the ancient Roman forum, this sculpture was a gift from the Italian government.

The garden slopes by hillside terraces to the lower boulevard, where a semicircular, brick-paved court forms a parapet and retaining wall. Here is set a double shell fountain, and the wall is decorated with six medallions of carved stone representing six great Italians whose genius has enriched the world. These are Giotto (1267-1337), Florentine artist regarded as the founder of modern art; Michelangelo (1475-1564), sculptor, painter, creator of the Sistine chapel murals, most famous artist of the Renaissance and perhaps of all time; Petrarch (1304-1374), Italian poet, Latin scholar, and great humanist Giuseppe Verdi (1813-1901), composer of the most popular operas ever written; Leonardo da Vinci (1452-1519), most typical genius of the Renaissance in his supremacy in the fields of painting, sculpture, architecture, music, science, engineering, and natural philosophy; and Guglielmo Marconi (1874-1937), Italian inventor, founder of commercial wireless telegraphy and of radio as we know it today.

The Italian Garden was formally opened on October 12, 1930, with the joint celebration of Columbus Day and the 2000th anniversary of the birth of the poet, Virgil, when the bust of the great poet was unveiled. Festivities began at nine oclock in the morning of the mild October day. Three thousand members of Italian societies heard extolled the rich cultural contributions of the Latin races to American civilization. A letter of congratulation to the City of Cleveland upon this occasion from Senatore Nobile Giacomo de Martino, royal Italian ambassador in Washington, read in part: "By honoring Virgil, Cleveland honors herself. Rome, capital of Latinity and jealous custodian of Latin culture, has appreciated the noble gift of this city. In response to the generous act with which the citizens of Cleveland have offered to the Italian community as a symbol of friendship and in memory of the Latin poet, a part of her public park to be dedicated to Virgil, Rome has sent a pedestal. This column has been handed down to us through the centuries, and perhaps has been witness to the triumph of the poet."

At noon on this day, a semi-circle of American, Italian, and fraternal banners was formed around the pedestal, and to the strains of band music, the bronze, laurel-crowned head of the gentle and beloved poet, was unveiled.

A message of congratulations from Herbert Hoover, then President of the United States, was read.

City Manager William R. Hopkins then spoke, stressing the cultural significance of these nationality gardens. Dr. John A. Barricelli delivered an address on Virgil in Italian, and Professor John Belfi a tribute in Latin. Commander Hugo Dudone, Italian war veteran of New York, compared the legacies to America of Virgil and Columbus. Count Cesare George B. Gradenigo, Italian Consul, then presented the bust, and Mayor John D. Marshall accepted it for the city. Mr. B. D. Nicola was master of ceremonies.

The executive committee in charge of a city-wide Virgil observance included Professor J. H. Hanford, Professor Clarence P. Bill, Mrs. Frances Bushea, Miss Mildred Chadsey, Miss Linda A. Eastman, Philip Garbo, Rossiter Howard, Dr. E. B. de Sauze, Leo Weidenthal, Charles J. Wolfram, and Mrs. Jennie K. Zwick. A plaque bearing a Virgil verse was presented to the garden during this celebration.

In 1932 Cleveland received from Italy a block of stone hewn from the side of Monte Grappa in northern Italy, in honor of the many northern Ohio members of the 332nd Regiment of Infantry, who fought on Italian soil in 1918. Here also is a tablet recalling the late General Balbos flight from Rome to Chicago in 1933.

Count Gradenigo, Mayor Marshall, Philip Garbo

In August of 1934, the Right Reverend Monsignor Edidio Vagnozzi, Papal delegate from Rome, in Cleveland for the Holy Rosary Church celebration of the Feast of the Assumption, visited the Italian Garden.

At the Columbus Day celebration in 1935, two bronze tablets were presented to the Italian Cultural Garden Association by its president, Mr. Philip Garbo. These tablets are affixed to the massive stone piers flanking the main garden entrance on the upper boulevard level. On one tablet are the names of one hundred famous Italians, the Italian coat of arms, and a raised map of Italy. On the other are two figures representing Italy offering America the fruits of her cultural achievement.

Speakers at the event included Dr. Romeo Montecchi, Italian Consul; Mrs. Josephine Novario, teacher of Italian at John Hay High School and the Cleveland Institute of Music; Mrs. G. A. Barricelli; Dr. C. Menzalora, and Charles J. Wolfram, then president of the Cleveland Cultural Garden League. Monsignor Joseph N. Trivisino, pastor of the Holy Rosary Church, placed a wreath in honor of Christopher Columbus.

In 1936 the Cleveland spring season of the San Carlo Opera Company was sponsored by the Cultural Garden League. The Italian Cultural Garden Association took a leading role in arranging for this festival of all-Italian operas.

On September 14, 1941, the completed Italian Cultural Garden was officially dedicated in a program honoring the garden as a symbol of the contribution of Italian culture to American democracy. Patriotic songs were sung by the assembled crowd, and Angelo Vitales band played.

A.L. De Maioribus, at that time president of the City Council, was principal speaker. His theme, addressed to free Americans, was "Strength Without Hatreds." In his address he pointed out that "nothing can be more disruptive of national unity than the importation of antagonisms of old Europe into our new world."

The Italian Garden was begun in 1939 and completed in 1941. The city contributed $18,061, and the Federal Government, in W.P.A. funds, $94,557, toward its total cost.

Officers through the years include Philip Garbo as president; Charles Cavano, first vice president; Federico Santi, second vice president; Mrs. Pauline Bruno, secretary, and Philip Garbo, Mrs. G. A. Barricelli, Eugene Palermo, and Frank Sancetta, trustees. The late Frank D. Celebrezze, brother of Mayor Anthony J. Celebrezze served the Italian Cultural Garden Association for many years as treasurer.

Lower Terrace Wall of the Italian Cultural Garden

The president executive committee of the Italian Cultural Garden consists of Philip Garbo, Judge B. D. Nicola, S. Cirelli, Anthony J. Celebrezze, A.L. DeMaioribus, F. Santi, John J. Locuoco, Folco Zugaro, Mr. and Mrs. John Garmone. Philip Garbo is president. Natale Comella is secretary.

The beautiful Italian Garden in the glorious Renaissance tradition it represents, forms a resplendent unit in the Cultural Gardens chain, and is a timeless asset to Cleveland and to America.

Upper Boulevard Entrance to the Italian Cultural Garden

Jugoslav Cultural Garden
City of Cleveland Photograph

Jugoslav Cultural Garden

The Jugoslav Cultural Garden is located near the St. Clair Avenue-East Boulevard approach to Rockefeller Park, and embodies the culture of the Slovenes, Croats, and Serbs. A circular fountain and pool are the central features of a paved court. Two stately linden trees, the typical Slovenian "lipa", whose sweet-scented, delicate blossoms are used in the brewing of a delightful tea, tower at either side of the garden entrance. The Jugoslav Garden slopes in three levels between the upper and lower boulevards. To the left of the entrance is a reposeful, formal, sunken garden to the right, a semi-circular section. A semi-circular stairway leads to the halfway lower level, and a wide stairway from the mid-level to the lower level, where there extends a spacious, stage-like paved court. Encircling this setting is a beautiful, natural amphitheatre formed of massive shade trees and the cooling stream of Doan Brook. Because of its theatre-like design, and the generous sweep of its lovely vistas, the Jugoslav Garden, since 1949, has provided the ideal setting for the annual One World Day celebrations. Over 2000 plants and flowering shrubs adorn this impressive garden.

The Jugoslav Cultural Garden was officially opened on May 15, 1938, with a parade of assembly of lodges, drill teams, and bands, and the presence of Dr. Adlesic, Mayor of Ljubljana, as principal speaker. Other speakers included Mr. John Mihelich, Mayor Harold H. Burton, Governor Martin L. Davey, Senator Robert Bulkley, Common Pleas Judge Frank J. Lausche, United States Representatives Martin L. Sweeney, Robert Crosser and Anthony Fleger; Chief Ohio Supreme Court Justice Carl V. Weygandt, Common Pleas Judge Frank J. Merrick, WPA Director Colonel Joseph H. Alexander, Hugo Varga, director of parks, Mr. Charles Wolfram, then president of the Cultural Garden League, Mrs. Marian Kuhar, treasurer of the Jugoslav Cultural Garden, Joseph Grdina, secretary of the Jugoslav Cultural Garden and Dr. Konstantin Fotic, Jugoslav Envoy in Washington. Mr. Anton Grdina was program leader.

The Jugoslav Cultural Garden group was organized in 1929. The first president was Councilman John Mihelich. Mr. Anton Grdina succeeded him, and has remained president to the time of this writing. Other officers active since the time of the gardens inception till the present are: Mr. Joseph Grdina, secretary; Mrs. Marian Kuhar, treasurer; and Mrs. Johanna Mervar, vice president. Mr. Anton Grdina has been the moving spirit, both from a material and cultural standpoint, of the Jugoslav Cultural Garden, and also has been actively interested in the entire Cultural Garden project, serving as treasurer, from its earliest period.

Anton Grdina at the Cankar Memorial

The site of this garden had been formally dedicated December 4, 1932, upon the occasion of the 14th anniversary of Jugoslav independence, for in 1918 Jugoslavia became a united kingdom after 17 centuries of struggle. Charles J. Wolfram presided at the ceremonies. Dr. Leonide Pitamic, Jugoslav Minister to the United States, professor of constitutional and international law, member of the Jugoslav delegation to the League of Nations, was the principal speaker. In his dedicatory remarks, he emphasized the equal importance of cultural and political international good will, and presented and planted an evergreen tree. Mrs. Jennie K. Zwick and Mr. Anton Grdina also spoke.

In the fountain rotunda are the busts of Bishop Frederick Irenaeus Baraga and the poet, Petar Petrovich Njegosh. The bust of Bishop Baraga was unveiled by the Slovenes on September 22, 1935. It was dedicated by Archbishop Dr. Gregory Rozman of Ljubljana, Slovenia. Guests of honor were Governor Martin L. Davey, and Dr. Bozidar Stojanovic of the Jugoslav Legation in Washington. Bishop Baraga was born in Slovenia in 1797, and was ordained a priest in 1823 after studies in Ljubljana (capital of Slovenia) and Vienna. In 1830 he came to America and was sent by the Archbishop of Cincinnati to the Ottawa Indians in the wilds of Michigan. He labored unstintingly against great physical and spiritual odds for the welfare of early Americans. Called the Apostle of the Chippewas and acclaimed a hero of the Northwest Territory, he also achieved fame as writer both in America and Europe.

This saintly man died on June 19, 1868, and is now being proposed for canonization in the Catholic Church.

The bust of their great poet, Petar Njegosh (1813-1851) was placed here by the Serbs of Cleveland. A distinguished statesman and philosopher, Njegosh was Prince-Bishop of Montenegro, and the first Montenegrin ruler who obtained recognition for Montenegro as an independent state. What Shakespeare is to the English, Njegosh is to the Serbs. His work attracted wide attention and was admired by Goethe. He is best known for his two epic poems, "The Mountain Garland" and "Light of the Microcosm".

Inscribed on the mounting of his bust in the Jugoslav Garden are these lines in English translation from one of his poems:

"flash mid mortal dust are we

We are a torch engirt by darkness.

What good is Empire to inhuman men,

Except to spread their shame through all the world.

The very corn is spiked for self-defense

And thorns do punish plucking of a rose.

The oppressed do rise against the oppressor

The stroke calls forth a flash from out the stone

Lacking that stroke, imprisoned were the spark.

Suffering reveals the virtue of the cross

Except by death was never Resurrection.

For all this vast array of things confused

Hath yet some rhythmic harmony and law:

Oer all this curious mixture of a world

There yet doth reign one over-arching Mind."

The priest, Simon Gregorcic (1844-1906) is the most beloved of all their poets to the Slovene people. The melody, the tenderness, the intensity, the heart-to-heart messages of his poems were a hopeful consolation to the oppressed people, who hailed their cheerful prophesies with great joy. An ethical note pervades much of his poetry, and because of their lyrical quality his poems readily lend themselves to musical settings. Many of them have become virtually folk-songs. A good example of his strong humanitarian feeling is conveyed in his poem, "Alone."

"Alas for him who sighs in grief alone

Nor happy he who drinks his joys alone.

Is Heaven kind to thee, O brother mine,

Then from thy fellows turn not eyes of thine.

The noble mind all pain alone will bear,

But happiness will with another share.

Thy heart, thy hand wide open lay,

And seek to wipe a brothers tear away,

Seek thou an orphans sorrow to allay.

He who would drink his joys alone,

Shall shed his tears in grief alone."

The 100th anniversary of the birth of Simon Gregorcic* was commemorated by the Jugoslav Cultural Garden group on August 13, 1944. The program featured a colorful pageant and some of the poets finest works.

Archbishop Rozman at Unveiling of Baraga Bust

In a small court to the right of the fountain rotunda is the bronze head of Ivan Cankar, also honored as an immortal poet by the Slovenian people. He was born in 1876 in Vrhnika, Slovenia, and died in 1918 at Ljubljana. The Cankar and Gregorcic monuments were jointly dedicated on August 13, 1944, by two Slovenian professors, Dr. France Trdan, Superintendent of Schools, and Professor Julius Slapsak, both of Ljubljana.

Cankar is an emotional, subjective writer, revealing a profound symbolism. He freely employs allegory, paradox, and satire, but only as a means of emphasizing the truth as he sees it. He is often a negative writer, succumbing to a bitter pessimism, but this is his method of bringing out the more forcibly his deep yearning and his unswerving faith in his people, spurring them on to greater activity in the attaining of right and justice. The bronze head of Ivan Cankar in the Jugoslav Garden is the work of Rudolph Mafko, the only Slovene sculptor in the United States.

Each year, the Serbs hold their own celebration in the Jugoslav Garden.

The statehood of Jugoslavia, constructed out of the ruins of the Austro-Hungarian monarchy, dates from the close of the First World War. The homeland of the Jugoslavs included former subjects of Austria-Hungary, Serbia, and Montenegro. Their union and independence were achieved in 1918. The Slovenes, Croats, and Serbs, throughout history have been very closely bound by ethnic and linguistic bonds, yet, because of divergent backgrounds—the Slovenes and Croats under western, the Serbs under eastern influences—show marked political and cultural differences.

Substantial material and cultural progress was made by the new state during the two decades before the

Second World War. Autonomy, democracy, and constitutionalism were near fulfillment at the dark and chaotic time of the Nazi invasion in 1941.

In addition to their might contribution to labor, which has helped to make America the most prosperous nation in the world, Americans of Jugoslav origin have added the gifts of their honesty, their thrift, their genial and quaint hospitality, and their strong moral consciousness. The fusion of these qualities with the best in American ideals and traditions insures a high type of citizenship.

The Jugoslav Cultural Garden is the concrete testimony of the stubborn idealism of this brave people, and of their love of their national poets and of their adopted country.

*Translation by Ivan Zorman. Cleveland poet and musician of Jugoslav descent, who contributed the major portion of this chapter.

Njegosh

Lithuanian Cultural Garden
City of Cleveland Photograph

Lithuanian Cultural Garden

The Lithuanian Cultural Garden extends between the upper and lower East Boulevard, commanding an inspiring view from both levels, and constructed in the shape of a large lyre, emblematic of the Lithuanian love for music in which, through centuries of national oppression, the Lithuanian people has expressed both its sorrows and its joys.

The stone work in this garden portrays three epochs of Lithuanian history.

The unification of the three Lithuanian provinces or tribes under the rule of the Grand Duke Gediminas at the beginning of the fourteenth century—an event which inaugurated an era of pride and strength for the

Lithuanian nation—is represented by a sculptured wall in the lower garden. A reproduction of a three-pillared symbolic piece of sculpture built by Gediminas to commemorate Lithuanian unity in the City of Vilnius in ancient Lithuania, it stands as a memorial to Lithuanias past greatness.

Another stage in Lithuanian history is symbolized by the large stone Fountain of Biruta, the central feature of the upper boulevard level of the garden. It represents the era of pagan worship of the country before the Christianizing of Lithuania. Biruta, Grand Duchess and first Queen of Lithuania, was, according to legend, the daughter of a fisherman. Consecrated a vestal virgin to the goddess Praurime, whose shrine stood on a lofty mound overlooking the shore of the Baltic Sea, Biruta, when on the verge of becoming a priestess to the goddess, was seen by Keistutis, the son of Gediminas, who had stopped at the shrine to give thanks to the goddess on his return from battle with the Crusaders in Prussia.

On beholding Biruta, he fell in love with her and bore her away with him to make her his wife. Their son, Vytautas the Great, in 1410 defeated the Crusaders at Gruenwald. After this event, Lithuania voluntarily espoused Christianity.

Biruta is revered by the Lithuanian people as an ideal of feminine virtue, and many little Lithuanian daughters have been proudly named in her honor.

By implication, an emblematic fire is assumed to illuminate the Biruta Fountain, symbol of the everlasting flame kept by the vestal virgins in the pagan temple of old Lithuania.

The Fountain of Biruta is dedicated to the Lithuanian women of Cleveland, and bears a plaque testifying to their generous contributions and enterprising fund-raising which have made this monument possible.

A unique and fascinating feature of the Lithuanian Garden, also traceable to pagan influence, is the zig-zag motif used as a decorative theme. This symbolizes lighting in honor of Perkunas, ancient god of thunder, once worshipped in Lithuania.

The third stage of Lithuanian history—that of its rebirth after the First World War, is commemorated in the stone-paved lower court of the garden by a bust of Dr. Jonas Basanavicius (1851-1927), scholar, historian, and first president of the Lithuanian Republic in 1918. The bust is a gift of the Lithuanian Government.

In a nook of the upper level garden, which is planted with alleys of oak leaf and mountain ash, there is a bronze bust of Vincas Kudirka (1859-1899), poet, author, and composer of the Lithuanian national anthem. The Kudirka bust was erected by the Dr. Vincas Kudirka Society of Cleveland, and was dedicated on September 21, 1938.

On the opposite side of the garden, a nook has been appropriated for the placement of a bust of Maciulis Maironis, the poet-priest whose poems were the inspiration for the Lithuanians struggle for independence. Funds for this bust, at the present writing, are being raised by St. Georges Church.

Both the Basanavicius and Kudirka busts are copies of originals by Jonas Zikaras, now in the garden of the Museum of Kamas, Lithuania.

Also in the Lithuanian Garden are two oak trees, dedicated respectively to the Lithuanian Alliance of America and the Lithuanian Roman Catholic Alliance of America in appreciation for their large financial contributions and moral support in the building of the garden. A linden tree was dedicated to the Lithuanian Metropolitan opera star, Miss Anna Kaskas, whose concert yielded a contribution to the Lithuanian Garden sufficiently large to wipe out debts incurred during construction.

The original design was drawn up in Lithuania by Professor Dubinecras, and was modified to fit the boulevard topography by the City Plan Commission of Cleveland. WPA funds for the construction of the garden were approved to the amount of $27,000.

Basanavicius

The Lithuanian Garden was dedicated on October 11, 1936, with the unveiling of the statue of Dr. Jonas Basanaviciu. An impressive procession marched to the strains of the Lithuanian national anthem, and about 2000 spectators witnessed the ceremonies. A wreath of Lithuanian rue, red roses, and foliage of the diemedis, or Gods tree, was placed before the bronze statue by ladies in Lithuanian national costume.

Principal speaker was Bronius K. Balutis, Lithuanias Minister to the United States.

"Aside from being a picturesque lesson on the origins of the diverse population of this city, the Cultural Gardens development offers also an excellent course in international relations," Mr. Balutis said. " It is an encouraging sight to see a great municipality actually demonstrating that its citizens may speak many different tongues, may have many distinct customs, may be partisans of various political or religious beliefs—and still be peacefully united in a common purpose, for a common and noble achievement."

Mr. Balutis also spoke on behalf of his government in the Lithuanian language. K. S. Karpius, editor of Dirva, Lithuanian weekly, and the Reverend Vincent G. Wilkutatis of St. Georges Catholic Church, also spoke in Lithuanian.

Mayor Ray T. Miller accepted the bust of the Lithuanian hero on behalf of the city. Mrs. John L. Mihelich, first vice-president of the Lithuanian Cultural Garden Federation, together with Mrs. Lottie Sukys, secretary, unveiled the statue. Mrs. Mihelich also acknowledged the co-operation of the nineteen Lithuanian societies which worked to establish the garden.

Kudirka

Other distinguished visitors to the Lithuanian Garden, in addition to Mr. Balutis, Minister Plenipotentiary to the United States, have included the late Antanas Smetona, President of Lithuania; Mikas Bagdonas, attache of the Lithuanian Embassy, and Mykolas Skipitas of Lithuania.

The Sportsmen of Lithuania also staged a basketball game with the local St. Georges Church team, for the benefit of the garden.

Funds for the garden were raised by a local cultural committee and by the Cultural Garden Federation by sponsoring picnics, concerts, theatrical events, and bazaars; and by solicited contributions through individuals and the contributions of twenty-one affiliated clubs and societies in the Lithuanian Cultural Garden Federation. In this manner, $11,000 was raised.

The first meeting of the Lithuanian Cultural Garden Association occurred on October 4, 1929. The first officers were Vincent P. Chesnul, president; John T. Kerichter, first vice-president; Mrs. John L. Mihelich, second vice-president; K. S. Karpius, executive secretary; and Peter P. Muliolis, treasurer.

Officers at the present writing are John Brass, president; Florionas Saukevicius, first vice-president; Joseph Grazulevicius, second vice-president; Mrs. John L. Mihelich, recording secretary; and Mrs. Justin Mischik, financial secretary.

Active members who have contributed generously of their time and efforts through the years since the beginnings of Lithuanian Garden history, have been Mrs. John L. Mihelich and Mrs. Justin Mischik, both continuous office-holders in the Lithuanian League and its parent organization, the Cultural Garden Federation. Mrs. Mihelich is also president of the Womens Committee of the Cultural Garden Federation. Mrs. Pola Glugodas has been active as a tireless publicity chairman, and in fund raising since the gardens inception. Mr. V. P. Chesnul, first president, rendered outstanding service during the planning and dedication of the garden. Mr. John Brass has ably succeeded him as president. Mr. Peter P. Muliolis has served on the board since its inception, in charge of organization finances. Mr. K. S. Karpius, secretary, has successfully secured contacts with Lithuania and aid from the Lithuanian government, for the benefit of the garden. Mr. George Vensluvas, successor to Mr. Karpius, deserves credit for his direction of the Lithuanian Sportsmens show. Mr. Joseph Blaskevicius has led committees raising largest amounts in funds.

By such loyal efforts as these, has the beautiful Lithuanian Garden been added to the Cultural Garden chain.

*Panoramic View of Lithuanian Cultural Garden
from Lower Boulevard*

Polish Cultural Garden
City of Cleveland Photograph

Polish Cultural Garden

The Polish Cultural Garden, completed in 1935 and dedicated in 1934, is located on the Upper Boulevard at St. Clair Avenue. A hexagonal sunken court encircled by granite walls, the Polish Garden contains colorful flower-beds, privet and evergreen, and many shrubs and trees imported from Poland, including a tree from Chopins Polish estate. Graceful walks lead to the upper level, and a handsome stairway at the back of the Polish Garden leads to the lower level of the garden chain. An octagonal fountain is the central feature.

The site of the Polish Garden was dedicated on October 28, 1934, with the setting out of an elm tree from Poland. County Judge Frank A. Piekarski of

Pittsburgh was principal speaker. "Long before America was discovered," he said in part, "Poland had universities and was leading in world education. Long before Englands Magna Charta was forced on the king, Poland had freedom of religion and freedom of speech. The purpose of this garden is better to acquaint not only the American people, but others, with the quality of Polish culture."

Park Director August J. Kurdziel extended the greetings of the city administration, and paid tribute to the genius of Chopin, later to be honored in this garden, as "thoroughly Polish and yet international, and thus for Polish art a perfect ambassador to the rest of the world." Music was by the Harmonia Chopin Singing Society and the Ohio Circle of Polish Singers. Other speakers were Charles J. Wolfram, at that time president of the Cultural Garden Federation, Dr. I. M. Jarzynski, former president of the League of Polish Organizations, and Mrs. Mary Mondzelewski, chairman of the Leagues garden committee. Councilman E. P. Lewandowski was master of ceremonies.

Five busts of immortal Poles, mounted upon marble pedestals, are placed in the outer circle of the garden. A bronze bust of Ignace Jan Paderewski (1860-1941), world renowned pianist, patriot, statesman, and former Premier of Poland, occupies a place of honor. The bust was donated in 1947 by the Polish Army Veterans Association, Post No. 6. It was cast and sculptured by Amos Mazzolini, Antioch College professor.

A bust of Frederic Chopin (1810-1849), Polish composer and pianist of world renown, the centennial of whose death was recently commemorated throughout the world, was modeled by Charles Dienes, Cleveland artist, and was the gift in 1947 of Harmonia Chopin Singing Society.

The Paderewski and Chopin busts were jointly dedicated on June 22, 1947. The program was sponsored by the Polish Army Veterans Association, Post No. 6, and the Harmonia Chopin Singing Society. Biographies of Paderewski and Chopin were given by Francis X. Swietlik of Chicago, Chairman of the Polish Relief committee of the United States and dean of Marquette University Law School. The busts were accepted by Mayor Thomas A. Burke and Charles J. Wolfram. Mayor Burke hailed the world greatness of the two Polish artists. Felix Matia, chairman of the Board of Elections, also spoke. Z. P. Zakrzewski, commander of the Polish Army Veterans Association, opened the program. Stanley Olsztyn, head of the singing society, presided. The two busts were unveiled by the little Misses Joan Kupniewski and Barbara Zakrzewski, aged seven and nine respectively.

The bronze bust of Maria Sklodowska Curie (1867-1934), the worlds outstanding woman scientist, pioneer in research with radio-active substances, co-discoverer of radium and polonium, and Nobel Prize winner in physics in 1903 and chemistry in 1911—was donated in 1949 by the American Polish Womens Club. The Curie bust is the work of Frank L. Jirouch, and was dedicated on June 5, 1949. Mayor Thomas A. Burke, in accepting it for the city, cited Cleveland as an example to the world that various racial groups can live in peace and friendship. Mrs. Leo Orlikowski gave the address of welcome. Mrs. Thomas Curlanis sang the Star Spangled Banner. The bust was unveiled by Mrs. Felicia Kwiatkowski, chairman of the Curie fund. Mrs. Marie Rosinski made the formal speech of presentation. Dr. Chester R. Lulenski, reviewed Madame Curies life, and paid tribute to her as a good mother as well as a great scientist.

Chopin

Also honored here in Henryk Sienkiewicz (1846-1916), Nobel Prize winner for literature in 1905, dramatist and author of world-wide reputation, writer of numerous historical novels, including Quo Vadis, The Knights of the Cross, and The Trilogy. The bronze bust of Sienkiewicz was given in 1947 by the Polish National Alliance and was unveiled on July 3, 1949. Dr. Arthur Coleman, president of Alliance College, Cambridge Springs, Pennsylvania, principal speaker at the dedication ceremony, emphasized Sienkiewiczs world message of the triumph of Christianity over paganism, as vividly pictured in his novel, Quo Vadis. Governor Frank J. Lausche also paid tribute to Sienkiewiczs wisdom in pointing out a path for the world to follow, and Mayor Thomas A. Burke, in accepting the bust for the city, expressed deep gratitude for the great contributions of the Polish people to America. The bust was unveiled by P. Kozlowski of Chicago, vice-president of the Polish National Alliance.

In 1952 the bust of the noted Polish poetess, Maria Konopnicka, was unveiled and dedicated. This was the gift of the Polish Ladies Educational Circle.

On September 13, 1953, a solid bronze fountain with allegorical figures representing music, literature, science, and astronomy, an ornamental upper border of jumping fish, and small carved turtles at the base, the work of Sculptor Amos Mazzolini, was dedicated as a tribute to Polish arts in the flower-bordered rotunda of the Polish Garden, by a colorful procession of donors, members of St. Casimirs Parish, and boy and girl scouts, dancers, choral groups, and bands. After the flag-raising by the color guard, the singing of the National Anthem by all present, address of welcome and presentation by Mrs. Marie Rosinski and Mrs. Victoria Tomkalski, and Mr. Z. P. Zakrzewski, program chairman and president of the Alliance of Poles of America, Monsignor A. A.

Radecki, pastor of St. Casimirs, invoked a blessing and thanked God for the beauty of the garden. The fountain was unveiled by Mary Ann Galowitz and Andrea Radzyminski, girls from Circuit No. 89 of the Polish National Alliance. Leo Weidenthal, president of the Cultural Garden League, then accepted the fountain as a valued addition to the Cultural Gardens, which he described as the future heart of the City of Cleveland. Greetings of Mayor Thomas A. Burke were extended by Chief City Prosecutor Bernard J. Conway. Folk dances entitled Flirtation and Carousel were then presented by a large group of girls from Circuit No. 89 of the Polish National Alliance, accompanied by Robert Supinski, accordion player. Polish songs, This Is My Country, and Spring, were sung by the combined male and ladies Moniuszko choruses. Common Pleas Judge Felix T. Matia delivered the principal address, in which he thanked the donors of the Polish Garden for the spirit which makes our country greater. A letter of Congratulation was read by Mrs. Victoria Tomkalski from Governor Frank J. Lausche. Mrs. Tomkalski also delivered the closing address.

The Polish Garden represents the efforts of the Polish-American groups organized in 1928. The Broadway-Southeast group consists of Judge Joseph F. Sawicki (also vice-president of the Cultural Garden Federation), Mrs. Walter Modzelewski, Mrs. Felicia Kwiatkowski, Zygmunt Dybowski, Mrs. John Chojnacki, Mrs. Leo Orlikowski, E. P. Lewandowski, and Mrs. Joseph F. Sawicki.

Eastside group, organized by the community located between Superior and St. Clair Avenues, west of Ansel Road, is composed of the Right Reverend Monsignor A. A. Radecki, Judge Felix T. Matia, Z. P. Zakrzewski, Mrs. Marie Rosinski, Mrs. John S. Skowronski, Mrs. John Karpinski, and Mrs. M.

Zabkowski. Required funds were raised by appeals at group meetings, card parties, and the generous contributions of organizations and individuals, including penny donation of children from Catholic Polish Schools.

For centuries, Poland was the buffer state that protected the culture, the religion and the very existence of many peoples of Europe against Asiatic aggression.

Her kings, statesmen and educators played an important part in the cultural and political life of Europe.

The first Polish settlers came to this country in 1608 with Captain Smith and became members of the Virginia Company. There are now in this country about seven million Polish descendants.

Cleveland has about 150,000 residents of Polish ancestry. Some have resided here since about 1840. Dr. Mary E. Zakrzewski, of Cleveland, in 1856, was the first woman physician admitted to the practice of medicine in America.

The Polonaise Arts Club of Cleveland, has established a scholarship at the Cleveland Institute of Art, open to the most deserving student, regardless of color, religion or racial origin.

Richard Anuiszkiewicz, Polonaise Arts Club member, was recently awarded the Pulitzer Prize in painting. There are twenty-five artists of Polish descent who participate yearly in the May show at the Museum of Art and in the Polonaise Club annual exhibitions.

Judge Joseph F. Sawicki, in an address on the Polish Garden in November 1953, said: "The Cleveland Cultural Gardens, together with the Polish Garden are symbolic of hope, that the day may dawn when jealousy, suspicion, hatred, and strife may forever cease and be supplanted by universal peace and friendship among all the peoples of the world. They are the expression of the hope, that the culture of nations may never be ruthlessly destroyed, but instead, reverently preserved as a sacred heritage for all posterity."

Mme. Curie

Rusin Cultural Garden
City of Cleveland Photograph

Rusin Cultural Garden

The Rusin Cultural Garden, on the upper and lower East Boulevard, between the Czech and Slovak Gardens, is the fourth garden in succession from the East Boulevard and St. Clair intersection. Set in a wooded glade sloping down to the lower boulevard by way of a spacious terrace overlooking Doan Brook, it has a sandstone terrace with parapets of brick and stone on the upper level. The Rusin Garden is sponsored by the Rusin Cultural Garden Association, headed by Reverend Joseph Hanulya, pastor of Holy Ghost Greek Catholic Church.

Plans for the Rusin Garden were drawn up and approved in 1938. Chief supporter of the Rusin Garden movement was the Rusin Educational Society, with the Reverend Joseph P. Hanulya as president, Dr. Eugene Mankovich as vice-president, Michael Surso as secretary, and Sig T. Brinsky as attorney.

The Rusin Garden plot was dedicated on June 25th, 1939. Ceremonies began with a parade led by the Cathedral Latin High School Band. The opening address was by the Reverend Joseph P. Hunalya, president of the Rusin Cultural Garden Association, who alluded to the spot as a "shrine to the culture of all Rusins," as their garden joined the 28 other nationalities represented in the Cultural Garden League. The Garden site was blessed by the guest of honor, the Right Reverend Bazil Takach of Pittsburgh, Bishop of the Greek Catholic diocese of America. Bishop Takach led the litany, and in his address to the assemblage of over 1000 people of Rusin descent from Cleveland and Northern Ohio, urged, "with all your attention to the culture of your ancestors, do not forget to be loyal to this, our adopted country." Mayor Harold H. Burton expressed the wish for the continuance of Rusin culture in the city, because "Cleveland knows too little about your people and would like to know more." Dr. P. I. Zeedick, representative of the Greek Catholic Rusin Union of Pittsburgh reviewed the history of the oppressed Rusin people, and their noble struggle to preserve the elements of their ancient national culture. The Reverend Joseph Jackanich of Youngstown spoke about Alexander Duchnovich, Carpatho-Rusin poet. Other speakers were John W. Bricker, governor of Ohio, and Dr. Hugo Varga, director of Cleveland parks. National anthems and sacred chants were rendered by the combined choirs of Holy Ghost and St. Gregorys Greek Catholic Churches. At a banquet at Guildhall, Builders Exchanged Building, following the dedication, plans for the further development of the Rusin Garden were discussed by members and officers of the Rusin Cultural Garden Association.

Father Alexander Basil Duchnovich

On May 25, 1952, a bust of Father Alexander Basil Duchnovich was unveiled in the Rusin Garden by Father Joseph Hanulya. Msgr. Tomislav Firis, pastor of St. Nicholas Parish, officiated at the ceremony. The work of Sculptor Frank Jirouch, the bust, at a cost of $1300, was made possible by donations contributed by those present at the Rusin Cultural Garden dedication in 1939. On it are inscribed the words, "I was, am, and always will be a Rusin" —written by Father Duchnovich when a political prisoner, as a reply to the court which offered him his freedom if he would renounce his Rusin tendencies. These words later became the nucleus of the Rusin National Anthem.

Father Duchnovich, Rusin priest, patriot, poet, educator, and author of the Rusin National Anthem, lived from 1803 to 1865. He is honored as the chief force in elevating the cultural standards of the Rusin people. Also distinguished as dramatist, historian, scholar, legislator, humorist, and philosopher, this priest in the Greek Catholic church consecrated his life to the enlightenment of his people, largely through writing and publishing books in the Rusin language. He carried on his dauntless struggle for universal education and a rebirth of the national spirit during a period of the darkest political, economic, and even moral eclipse. In addition to the National Anthem, he is famous for the Rusin national march, several primers for children, volumes of poems, plays and history, and—one of the most cherished treasures of the Rusin people—a prayer-book, "The Bread of the Soul."

Books Father Duchnovich defined as "selfless friends, faithful friends...a lighthouse in the darkness of doubts, an anchor in the tempests of passions." Father Duchnovich lives on, a hero in the truest sense, to his beloved Rusin people.

The Rusins are a Slavic race of Asiatic origin, from which stem the Russians and Ukrainians.

Prior to World War I, the Rusin people comprised a part of the Austro-Hungarian Empire in the main, the Rusins lived in the Carpathian mountains, and were at times called Carpatho-Rusins.

In governmental and ecclesiastical documents the Rusins there are sometimes called Ruthenians.

Bishop Takach at Rusin Garden Dedication
Photograph by James Mell

Subsequent to World War I and as the creation of the Republic of Czechoslovakia the Rusin state, Ruthenia, was established as a part of the new republic.

Ruthenia is the eastern state of the said Republic of Czechoslovakia, however, large Rusin communities are found in the state of Slovakia which is adjacent to Ruthenia on its west.

The faith of the Rusins is Catholic. The rite is the old Bizantine-Slovanik of the Catholic Church.

A conscientious, thrifty, and homeloving people, they have enriched Clevelands civic and cultural life by their love of independence and political liberty, by the splendid capella choirs of their fellow Byzantine rites churches, and by sharing with their fellow citizens the Rusin Cultural Garden and the great work of their national hero, Father Duchnovich.

The spirit of the Rusin people, their history and their background are mirrored in the lovely garden which they have established as a part of the Cleveland Cultural Garden chain.

Parade to Rusin Cultural Garden on Dedication Day
Photograph by James Mell

Slovak Cultural Garden
City of Cleveland Photograph

Slovak Cultural Garden

The Slovak Cultural Garden, modern in spirit, extends along three acres of Rockefeller Park between the upper and lower East Boulevard drives, with the Italian Garden as its southern, and the Rusin Garden as its northern neighbor. Stone steps at the entrance lead to a large forum with two wings for the placement of the bronze busts of the Reverend Stefan Furdek (1855-1915) and the Reverend Jan Kollar (1793-1852), against a background of privet hedge and European trees and shrubs. Both statues are the work of Sculptor J. Tenkacs. A sandstone terrace opens on to a spacious oval lawn. This typically Slovakian garden was designed by landscape architect, T. Ashburton Tripp.

Slovak Garden history began in 1929 when, under the acting chairmanship of Joseph Smolka, leaders in fraternal, civic, and cultural Slovak organizations conferred with City Manager William R. Hopkins, and with Charles Wolfram and Jennie K. Zwick, at that time president and executive secretary respectively of the Cleveland Cultural Garden Federation, for the purpose of inaugurating plans to join other nationality groups and establish a Slovak Garden. The Slovak Cultural Garden Association was formed, with Judge George S. Tenesy as president and Mr. Anna Mokris as secretary. Substantial funds were raised by donations, song festivals, by the Stefanik Singing Society, card parties in halls and private homes, and a colorful Old World Slovak fair held in Stas Hall.

On October 23, 1932, the first unit of the Slovak Garden was dedicated. With the aid of government funds, the garden was completed, and was dedicated on October 28, 1934, with the unveiling of the two bronze busts. The bust of the Reverend Furdek was the gift of the First Catholic Slovak Union, and that of Jan Kollar of the Slovak Evangelical Union and Lutherans of Cleveland.

Reverend Stefan Furdek, author and educatory, Cleveland Slovak leader, and pastor of Our Lady of Lourdes Catholic Church, was born in 1855 at Trstena, Slovakia. While completing his theological studies in Prague, he was selected as a seminarian at the request of Bishop Gilmore of the Cleveland Diocese. He was ordained for the priesthood in July of 1882, a few months after his arrival in America. For a short time he served as assistant at St. Wenceslaus Church, then was appointed first pastor of the newly organized parish, Our Lady of Lourdes, where his ministry lasted thirty-two years—until his death in 1915. Father Furdek, in addition to his pastoral duties, organized the First Catholic

Slovak Union and the First Slovak Ladies Union in 1889. He also wrote several books of outstanding literary merit, distinguished poems, scientific articles, instructive books and books dealing with entertainment, and a series of readers for Slovak schools in wide present-day use.

Jan Kollar was born in 1793 in Mosovche, Slovakia, of a family highly respected for its admirable character and inspiring community services. A Lutheran minister of high standing, Kollar fearlessly defended the scholastic and language rights of both Lutheran and Catholic Slovaks. His poetic masterpiece entitled, The Daughter of Glory predicted liberty and independence for the Slovaks. To his credit are the memorable words, "What hundreds of blundering ages prepared is changed by a single epoch."

Reverend Kollar

For many years an active fund campaign and cultural program were conducted under the presidency of Peter Mokris. The Slovak Cultural Garden Association also has had splendid cooperation and generous donations from William R. Hopkins, Monsignor F. J. Dubosh, Reverend John Krespinsky, Reverend M. F. Benko, Anthony Stas, James J. McGinty, Mr. and Mrs. Frank Misencik, Mr. and Mrs. George S. Tenesy, Mr. and Mrs. J. W. Kulka, Mr. and Mrs. Andrew Halko, Florian Zavasky, Mrs. Michael Beno, Zivena Beneficial Society, and Slovak Catholic Union. City Landscape Architect Thomas Jones, Parks Commissioner Sam Newman, and the Mayors and their administrations during the years of Slovak Garden history, are also gratefully acknowledged by the Slovak Garden group, which, from 1935 to 1941 raised the sum of $3,000 toward the completion of its garden. Materials were purchased with this money, and labor costs were paid from funds allotted by the Works Progress Administration through the City of Cleveland.

An elaborate celebration with a parade of all nationality groups took place in the Slovak Garden in July, 1939, when it was officially re-dedicated. During the period of the Second World War, the Slovak Cultural Garden Association transferred its activity to War Bond solicitation to an amount exceeding $50,000, and to patriotic national unity programs. In 1942, together with the First Catholic Slovak Union and the First Catholic Slovak Ladies Union, the Association sponsored a patriotic program during the Four Freedoms Festival. A playlet, The Dawn We Watch, was presented and attended by many national, state, and local officials.

In 1946, the Slovaks participated enthusiastically in the 150th anniversary of the founding of the City of Cleveland. In the One World Day Celebration on July 21st of that year, their beautiful parade float was awarded an honorable mention by the Sesquicentennial

Committee. On the following day, festivities continued with singing and dancing on the International Stage by the Stefanik Singing Society, which won the acclaim of an audience of 200,000 people. The first One World Day program was held in the Slovak Garden.

On May 1, 1936, the Slovak leaders of the Slovak Academy of Culture and Science of Slovakia planted a linden tree in the Slovak Garden, when Dr. Hronsky, secretary of the Academy, stated that only in a city like Cleveland and a national like the United States can groups function for inter-racial and inter-cultural understanding.

A Four Freedoms Festival held at Benedictine Hall on August 30, 1942, was attended by 3,000 people, including many outstanding political and cultural leaders. There was music by a concert orchestra.

Cleveland Slovaks played a prominent role in the Sesquicentennial celebration in 1946. The Slovak group took a large and hospitable part in the preview tea given for the benefit of the Sesquicentennial committee. The Slovak group float in the One World Day parade for July 25, 1946, was awarded honorable mention. A program of national Slovak music and dancing was later viewed with pleasure by many thousands of spectators.

On March 31, 1949, the Slovak group participated in the Unesco Convention. Mrs. Anna Mokris, whose faithful service as recording secretary of the Cultural Gardens Federations is well known, supervised the serving of delicacies, contributed by 24 nationality groups at the benefit tea given for some 3,000 delegates. Representatives of these groups wearing their beautiful native costumes supplied a colorful background. Here, too, the Slovak contribution was prominent.

The Second One World Day celebration was held in the Slovak Garden on July 20, 1948. Also, in June of that year, the Slovak group gave a tea for 200 Cleveland school teachers in the Slovak Garden.

Through the years prominent leaders from Slovakia, the Reverend Joseph Tiso, President of Slovakia, and a group of scientific and cultural leaders of the Academy of Science and Culture, have visited the Slovak Cultural Garden and planted trees and shrubs.

Present officers of the Slovak Cultural Garden Association are: Andrew E. Zolata, president; Mary Misencik, 1st vice president; Theresa Krajcer, 2nd vice president; Tillie H. Bacik, secretary; Peter Mokris, treasurer.

Thus has one more nationality group—the Cleveland citizens of Slovak descent—added another link to the Cultural Gardens chain. The city is grateful for this picturesque garden, and for the life works of the two great Slovaks who are honored here.

Reverend Furdek

Ukrainian Cultural Garden
Photograph by Spence

Ukrainian Cultural Garden

The Ukrainian Cultural Garden is located on the west side of the lower boulevard, opposite the Greek Garden level. Brick and stone courts are connected by paved walks to produce a richly formal effect in a background setting of varying shades of green. The entrance is to the left court through a stone and iron gateway bearing bronze plaques and portrait reliefs by Frank L. Jirouch, representing Bohdan Khmelnitsky (1593-1657), leader of a revolt against the Poles in 1614, and Mikhail Hrushevsky (1866-1934), historian, teacher, and author. Main interest centers around three bronze busts of famous Ukrainians—Ivan Franko (1856-1916), poet, patriot, and folklorist Volodimir the Great (956-1015), first Christian ruler of the Ukraine and Taras

G. Shevchenko (1814-1861), poet, teacher, reformer, liberator of Serfs in Russia whose popular poems have won him the name of the Father of Ukrainian Literature. These three busts are the work of Alexander Archipenko, world-famous master of modern art and one of the founders of cubism, who was born in Kiev, the ancient capital of Ukraine. These sculptures thus greatly enrich the art treasures of Cleveland.

The Ukrainian Garden was completed in 1939. By a City Proclamation, Mayor Harold H. Burton designated June 2, 1940, for the formal dedication of the Ukrainian Cultural Garden. "Whereas the Ukrainian Cultural Gardens form a strong and important link in the chain of the Cultural Gardens," the Proclamation read in part, " and whereas these Ukrainian Gardens are symbols of the contribution of the Ukraine to the cultural and spiritual development of the world...as mayor of Cleveland, I designate Sunday, June 2, 1940 as the day for the formal dedication of the Ukrainian Cultural Garden in Rockefeller Park, and I invite all who can do so to participate in the dedicatory exercises."

On June 1, 1940, an impressive and well-attended pre-dedication concert was given in the Music Hall of Public Auditorium. The famous National Chorus "Dumka" of Detroit, the Ukrainian Dancing Guild, and guest soloists, Maria Sokil, Olga Lepkovs, and Antin Rudnitsky, were featured. Mrs. Harold H. Burton extended greetings on behalf of her husband, the mayor.

The dedication ceremonies on June 2, 1940, were attended by over 8,000 persons, including many out-of-town guests. Professor Clarence A. Manning, head of the department of East European languages at Columbia University of New York City, delivered the principal address. Mayor Burton accepted the new garden on behalf of the city. Other speakers included Dr. Luke

Myshuha, editor of the Ukrainian daily "Svoboda," of New York, Archbishop Ivan Theodorovich of Philadelphia, and Charles Wolfram, then president of the Cultural Gardens Federation. Omer E. Miles, attorney, and president of the United Ukrainian Organizations, was chairman and master of ceremonies.

Volodimir the Great
Photograph by Dania Howykowycz

Governor John W. Bricker sent a message congratulating the United Ukrainian Organizations on their Cultural Garden undertaking, and expressing his conviction that the Ukrainian Garden would do much to acquaint citizens generally with Ukrainian history and with the achievements of Ukrainian scholars, writers, and poets.

The Ukrainian Cultural Garden was developed, with the aid of Federal and City grants, principally by the United Ukrainian Organizations of Cleveland a central council, composed of clubs, societies, and associations for the purpose of directing and encouraging cultural, educational, and welfare work among the 25,000 Ukrainians of Cleveland. This organization is affiliated with the Ukrainian Congress Committee of America, which strives to assist morally, politically, and financially, the liberation of Ukraine, and to attain its sovereignty. Its generous and tireless members and its enterprising executive board, composed of Omer E. Miles, John Spodar, Harry Stepanek, Dmytro Szmagala, William Wolansky, Theodore Haycey and Walter Woycitsky, have been largely instrumental in enriching Cleveland with this magnificent garden.

The home of the Ukrainian people is the vast and fertile prairie stretching from the Carpathian Mountains eastward to the Sea of Azov. Several rivers, of which the Dnieper is the largest, cross the country in the same general direction from north to south, running into the Black Sea or into the Sea of Azov. In the north the Ukrainians have expanded from the steppes to the forest zone, especially on the right bank of the Dnieper River, so there is no natural northern boundary to their country.

Nature has showered her gifts lavishly on Ukraine. The famous "black earth" (chornozem) is among the riches in the world, and since the end of the eighteenth century Ukraine has been known as the "granary of Europe".

Here the aboriginal Slavic tribes from which the Ukrainians descend lived from time immemorial. But while God favored the land with His gifts, man was not left to live there is peace and abundance. From prehistoric times, Ukraine has been a battlefield between east and west, north and south.

Shevchenko
Photograph by Dania Howykowycz

The Ukrainians have sometimes been termed "the Irish of the Slavonic World", and the epithet is not infelicitous. In both cases there is a tradition of ancient, almost legendary glory, followed by long centuries of stifled independence, in which the stream of national life disappeared underground almost completely—only to emerge in turbid and eager flood in modern times.

The Ukrainian language is an East Slavonic tongue which is closely akin to Russian but which differs from it very sharply in many important grammatical and phonetic ways. The language is spoken by a people of some forty millions in number who are almost wholly included in what is known as the Ukrainian Socialist Soviet Republic. Before the Second World War, the country was divided between the Soviet Union, Poland, Rumania and Czechoslovakia. Before the First World War, it was divided between Russia and Austria-Hungary.

The individuality of the Ukrainians as a people stands out clearly, despite conquerors efforts to assume their past, deny their present, and alter their future.

Franko
Photograph by Dania Howykowycz

Acknowledgements

The Cleveland Cultural Garden Federation is grateful to the many Clevelanders who responded to the public appeal for funds to aid in the publication of "Their Paths Are Peace."

Grateful acknowledgement for generous cooperation in the collecting and compiling of material for this book is made to the Executive Committee of the Cleveland Cultural Garden Federation composed of Leo Weidenthal, Mrs. Norma Wulff, Judge Louis Petrash, Judge Joseph F. Sawicki, Anton Grdina, Mrs. Lewis W. Phillips, Mrs. Frank Mervar, Mrs. Mary K. Duffy, Philip Garbo, George N. Kalkas to Mr. and Mrs. Peter Mokris for access to their complete files on the history of the Cultural Gardens to Frank Jirouch, Ivan Zorman, James C. Mylonas, Omer E. Miles, Lieutenant-Colonel Jack Persky, Judge Julius M. Kovachy, Stephen Gobozy, the Reverend Joseph Hanulya, S. T. Brinsky, Mary Ellen Murphy, Judge John V. Corrigan, Dr. Joseph Remenyi, Mrs. William Engelmann, Mrs. Mary Skowronski, Mrs. John L. Mihelich, Mrs. Marie Rosinski and many other active workers for the Cultural Gardens.

The Federation also desires to express its appreciation of the cooperation on the part of the City of Cleveland, through Parks Director John J. Locuoco and Commissioner of Parks Harold J. Lausche in supplying a large proportion of the pictures used in this work.

By authorization of the Cleveland Cultural Garden Federation, compilation and publication of "Their Paths Are Peace" were directed by the Executive Committee of the Federation. A special sub-committee in active charge consisted of Judge Louis Petrash, George N. Kalkas, Anton Grdina and Leo Weidenthal.

The Cleveland Cultural Garden Federation
Founded in 1926
For the Promotion of Brotherhood and Intercultural Understanding

President
Leo Weidenthal

Vice Presidents
Judge Louis Petrash
Judge Jos. Sawicki
Norma Wulff

Executive Secretary
Mrs. Lewis W. Phillips

Corresponding Secretary
Mrs. Frank Mervar

Treasurer
Anton Grdina

Financial Secretary
Mrs. George W. Mercer

Executive Committee Members
Mrs. Mary K. Duffy
Philip Garbo
George N. Kalkas

Decorative Drawings by B. H. Rosenbaum
Individual Drawings of the Cultural Gardens by John Csosz

Original Edition Printed in Cleveland, Ohio by Western Newspaper Printing and Matrix Company

About the "New" New Edition

This is the second time I have published this book. And, just like the first time, it feels a little strange writing an addendum — adding my words to a book that was published 65 years ago. But I needed to take a moment to answer some questions about this new edition.

What gives you the right to do this?

This book was originally published and copyrighted in 1954. At the time of the original publication, one of the requirements for copyright was, that for a work to remain in copyright, it needed to be renewed in its 28th year. The copyright was never renewed and so in the early 1980s the work fell into the public domain.

Why republish this book 65 years later?

During a planning meeting for the 2014 Cleveland One World Festival, an expansion of the Cultural Gardens' "One World Day" celebration, the book had been mentioned as a possible donor gift. While the contents of this book (scans and basic text conversion) are online both at *The Cleveland Memory Project* and on *Ebrary* - the physical book has long been out of print. As a publisher, I cringe at the words "out of print"; and as a Clevelander, who for the past 30 years has worked in University Circle and drives through the Cultural Gardens daily, I thought: **"Why not bring it back to life?"**

Why not a revision?

During the One World Festival planning meetings, people talked about the amount of change that has happened since 1954.

Lower East Boulevard is now Martin Luther King Boulevard and Upper East Boulevard is simply East Boulevard.

When this book was first published, there were only 16 gardens. Since 1954 the gardens have grown to include The Albanian Garden (2012), The Armenian Garden (2010), The Croatian Garden (2011), The Syrian Garden (2011), The Indian Garden (2005), The Finnish Garden (1958), The Estonian Garden (1966), The Latvian Garden (2006), The African American Garden (1977), The Romanian Garden (1967), The Azerbaijan Garden (2008), The Chinese Garden (1985), The Serbian Garden (2008), and, after the breakup of Yugoslavia, The Jugoslav Garden was renamed The Slovenian Garden.

This book doesn't need a revision — it needs a sequel! It is my sincere hope that the republishing of this book inspires someone to follow the path laid down by Clara Lederer to write the next chapter of the history of the Cultural Gardens of Cleveland. And if you do, I will publish it!

Why change the format?

The original book was published as a 99 page, 8½x11" hardcover, in a 2-column format. It is very academic in style, which makes for a difficult read.

The online versions of the book are either an exact replica of the printed pages or a scan & conversion of the book presented in a scholarly but not in a comfortable or friendly way.

This book needs to be enjoyed!

In 2014, I scanned an original (and pristine) copy of the book, cleaned up all the images, so they would reprint well, reassembled all of the text, and then redesigned the book without columns for an 8x8" square paperback that is 154 pages. The goal was to make the book as readable and accessible as possible. Many obvious typos were corrected but purposeful alternate spellings were left intact (such as theatre vs. theater).

In 2019, I finally got around to creating the eBook and realized that when I stylized the 8x8" square I had cornered myself and was going to have to redesign the entire book, again, to match the fluid nature of eBooks. And while the 8x8" format is poetic it isn't a standard and I decided (in honor of the 65th anniversary of the book) to not just create the eBook but to create a lovely mass-market 6x9" version (now 196 pages). If you own an 8x8" version – it is now a collectible!

I started a publishing company because I love bringing books to life and, if you are holding this book, you know the life contained within.

Jared Bendis
ATBOSH Media Ltd.
www.ATBOSH.com

The Cleveland Cultural Gardens
www.CulturalGardens.org

The Cleveland Cultural Gardens at
The Cleveland Memory Project
www.ClevelandMemory.org/gardens/
www.ClevelandMemory.org/ebooks/tpap

www.ingramcontent.com/pod-product-compliance
Lightning Source LLC
Chambersburg PA
CBHW070058080526
44586CB00013B/1110